NO AGENT NEEDED

The Hottest Tips, Tricks, and Hacks from Rockstar Real Estate Investors That Anyone Can Use to Sell Their Properties Fast and for Top Dollar without a Real Estate Agent

Created by
Matt Theriault

Contributions by
Billy Alvaro
Greg Zytkowski & Russell Taylor
Jeff Garner
Jason Hollon
Parker Stiles
Jeremiah Johnson
Paul Thompson
Todd Toback
Drew Hitt
Omar Merced
Stuart Gethner
Michael Fitzgerald
Nasar El-arabi
Raul Bolufe

Published by Best Seller Publishing®, Pasadena, CA
Best Seller Publishing® is a registered trademark
Printed in the United States of America.

This publication is designed to provide accurate and authoritative information with regard to the subject matter covered. It is sold with the understanding that the publisher is not engaged in rendering legal, accounting, or other professional advice. If legal advice or other expert assistance is required, the services of a competent professional should be sought. The opinions expressed by the authors in this book are not endorsed by Best Seller Publishing® and are the sole responsibility of the author rendering the opinion.

Most Best Seller Publishing® titles are available at special quantity discounts for bulk purchases for sales promotions, premiums, fundraising, and educational use. Special versions or book excerpts can also be created to fit specific needs.

For more information, please write:
Best Seller Publishing®
1346 Walnut Street, #205
Pasadena, CA 91106
or call 1(626) 765 9750
Toll Free: 1(844) 850-3500
Visit us online at: www.BestSellerPublishing.org

CONTENTS

INTRODUCTION

If you're reading this book, it's probably because you've been pondering the idea of selling a property, and various ideas have crossed your mind, like: (a) You might be able to maximize your profit by doing it yourself, (b) you might be able to avoid the interaction and the perceived costs that accompany working with a real estate agent, (c) you think you might be able to do it quickly because you happen to be in a hot market at the time you're reading this book, and/or (d) quite honestly, it just looks really easy—it ain't rocket science, or is it? Ha-ha, no, it's not. However! Experience has its benefits.

In some regards, with today's technology and advancement, transacting real estate is pretty simple. You can probably do this alone without a hitch. There are many different services available, whether marketing services, fulfillment services, or transaction services that can allow the average person to sell their house in a relatively short period of time—all of that is relative, pertaining to your definition of a successful sale and whatever the current market conditions dictate.

In terms of getting a good price for what you sell, it's possible, as long as you know what you're doing. But if you get this part wrong, you absolutely can spend too much time on the market—to the point where your property becomes an old-and-stale OPT (overpriced turkey) that nobody wants to look at anymore. At that, even with the offers you might eventually receive, those buyers recognize that you've been on the market for a long time, so they present you with lowball offers, thinking you're desperate. When the motivation behind an offer is more of an opportunistic one, it's tough to get a good and legitimate conversation with a buyer started.

Overall, if you choose to do this alone, there are legal ramifications that could potentially complicate things. There are national and federal disclosures to incorporate for your safety. There are statewide and even citywide disclosures that you need to be concerned about, as well. If you get this part wrong, it could cost you time and money; but if you get it right, then everything you envisioned for yourself when you picked up this book is also possible.

My name is Matt Theriault, and I am a real estate investor. I was previously a real estate agent for four years before I became a real estate investor. I've been a very successful one for the last twelve years; I have more than a thousand transactions under my belt—actually, I have many more than that (I stopped counting a long time ago). I haven't seen it all, but I've seen a lot, and that's why I know this can be done by the average person with a little bit of time, some experience (first or secondhand) and some attention to detail. I also know that this industry can be perceived as being much easier than it actually is. With that in mind, I wanted to write a book that gives you that option, and gives you enough information so you can make an educated decision about whether proceeding to sell your property without an agent is a good fit for you—or hiring an agent is the better route. It will primarily come down to what you value most, time or money. Would you rather have the fast nickel or the slow dime? There's no right-or-wrong, good-or-bad, answer to that question, by the way.

Needing to sell your house for top dollar or needing to sell it fast—these situations require two different approaches to selling a house, each necessitating their own mindset and strategy. The most common mistake people make when selling a house on their own occurs when applying a "fast-dime" strategy. The frequent result is a "slow nickel." I don't want to see that happen to you, so I dug into my network of some of the most experienced real estate investors in the country. I asked them to join me in this book and share their experience and expertise—particularly in the type of scenario you're probably envisioning right now: (a) selling seems like a really good idea, (b) you have a potential home run on your hands because of all the different things available to facilitate a sale without an agent, and (c) this looks like it's going to be something fantastic, and it very well could be.

So, I specifically asked my friends to come along and recall some past transactions and impart the lessons learned from a wide array of situations where they, too, were seemingly staring easy home runs in the face. Even with all their experience and available resources, random, wild pitches and foul balls took significant bites out of their run count. They've now shared their lessons learned along the way, as well as some of their regrets. Where they could have done things differently, they have shared that, too. I hope this will give you some good pointers and advice as to what you can watch out for as you approach selling your property on your own.

The names of my colleagues are as follows:

Billy Alvaro
Greg Zytkowski & Russell Taylor
Jeff Garner
Jason Hollon
Parker Stiles
Jeremiah Johnson
Paul Thompson
Todd Toback
Drew Hitt
Omar Merced
Stuart Gethner
Michael Fitzgerald
Nasar El-arabi
Raul Bolufe

So, those are my friends. They are experienced real estate investors from all across the country, who have a world of experience. Some of what they share might be a good fit for you; some of it might not. Consider their advice in each chapter as if you were looking at a clothing rack full of new coats. Try each one on, look in the mirror, and get a feel for it. Look yourself up and down, and stretch your arms a bit. It will be a comfortable fit that you enjoy, or it won't. If you like how it fits, buy it; go for it. If you don't like how it fits, put it back on the rack and move on to the next chapter for your next fitting.

I hope this book is helpful! Real estate is not an exact science. There are many moving parts and variables at play in every transaction. No one could be prepared for every possible scenario; however, I believe I put forth a valiant effort to prepare you.

I pulled from my colleagues as many different types of applicable scenarios as possible, especially their more dangerous, emotional, and expensive experiences. What I've compiled in this book is educational and practical (as well as entertaining at times), in the interest of minimizing the potential for loss while tipping the odds in your favor for the outcome you desire. An agent has their place in a real estate transaction, but they're certainly not required.

Enjoy!

ANOTHER NIGHTMARE ON ELM STREET

By
Billy Alvaro

Long Island

I am a serial entrepreneur, serving fellow Americans as far back as I can remember. In my young adult years, I served in the United States Air Force and then, as a Police Officer in Long Island, NY, where I realized my passion was real estate. In 1999, I started a mortgage bank which eventually employed over 950 associates. During this time, I was recognized as the Top 40 Business person under the age of 40 by *Long Island Business News*. Also, The Columbia Association awarded me Business Man of the Year, and *Inc 500 Magazine* named my company the 136th fastest-growing, privately held company in the US. Today, I own and operate Easy Sell Property Solutions, and Max Returns Real Estate Investments—the most successful real estate investment companies in New York.

Even though I'm dedicated to nurturing and growing my business and the teammates who support it, I'm also a big believer in balance. I have a love for people and life. I live as if each day is my last, and I encourage everyone to do the same. I practice daily meditation, and I'm seriously into health and fitness. I'm also a believer in and practitioner of the Law of *INCREASE*—an acronym that stands for Inspire, Never quit, Constant improvement, Respect, Excellence, Attitude, Systems, and Exponential:

> *Inspire* all with whom you come in contact to *do*, *be*, or *have* whatever they desire.

> *Never* quit, lie, or cheat.

> *Constant* and never-ending improvement.

Respect that you need to give to get.

Excellence in all we do.

Attitude will make or break you.

Systems rule!

Exponential growth.

The Elm Street Story

So, we received a call from a seller who found us on the Internet. He was looking to sell his home and was interested in working with us. And the next day we received a call from his wife who found us from one of our direct-mail campaigns. They were going through a divorce, and neither of them wanted to pay the mortgage or keep up with the maintenance of the house. Neither of them knew the other was calling because they weren't talking—at least not civilly. Both called because they had run out of time. Though the house was in a great location, it was about to be lost to a tax auction and was in pre-foreclosure with the bank. They had only two weeks before their house was to be auctioned and lost, along with all their equity.

We went out to the property on Elm Street to meet them, and it was a catastrophe—both of them were yelling and casting blame at each other for the condition of the house, as well as the issues with taxes and the town. The house was in terrible condition, practically falling apart, and loaded with items, a hoarder house—there were also about fourteen cats living inside. We spoke to each owner separately and were able to agree on a price that was fair for us and fair for them. Our primary concern was that we needed to move quickly so they wouldn't lose the equity they had in the home.

Both said they had tried to sell in the past, but couldn't find a buyer because of all the issues they had with each other and the house itself. Little did I know, previous buyers backed out for a reason—one not yet known to me. Well, after we signed the paperwork and got things moving, we realized just how many problems this property and its owners had:

1. Mortgage

2. Violations

3. Water damage (including mold)

4. Judgments on the sellers (attached to the property)

The first problem was the fact that they had not one mortgage, but two. Both were in default, and both lenders wanted their money immediately. They had multiple violations on the house: (a) an illegal apartment in the basement which hadn't been used in years, (b) too many cars without plates parked on the front lawn, (c) unhealthy conditions in the home, and (d) a rear dormer that didn't have a certificate of occupancy. I mean it looked like the town parked in front of their house and just wrote out every imaginable violation under the sun.

But the biggest problem we faced came to light when we found serious water damage and a sinking foundation in the rear of the home. The house was built in an area with a high water table, and every time it rained, the water table would rise, literally wicking up through the concrete floor and flooding the basement. This leaking lead to the rear wall being sunk and bowed in, and black mold was growing everywhere. We didn't see any of this when we first went into the home because there hadn't been rain for three weeks and there was a lot of stuff covering the whole basement. So, not only were we dealing with multiple mortgages, multiple violations, and a serious water/foundation problem, we also learned that both sellers had judgments against them attached to the property.

This very profitable dream deal, all of a sudden, looked more like a nightmare. There were many mistakes made with this purchase. Because of time constraints and the number of items in the home, we couldn't assess the condition of the house in the proper manner; still, we should have taken our time and assessed it thoroughly. After we sifted through all the title issues, additional mortgages, judgments, and back taxes, then reevaluated the structural issues, we put on our thinking caps to figure out how to resolve the issues in a way that would ensure the following:

1. The sellers wouldn't lose their house to the tax auction.

2. They would walk out with some cash.

3. We would get a house from which we could make a return on our investment without losing our shirt.

We showed the sellers that, under the current situation (with their judgments and additional mortgages), they wouldn't be able to sell their house and receive money at the closing. In fact, they would've needed to bring money to the closing table. I explained that, at the current purchase price, we (the buyers) would also lose money if we were to purchase it at the number upon which we originally had agreed, because of the structural and water problems.

Once I established the situation, I told them, "I think I have a solution for all of us to come out as winners."

I explained that our company, Easy Sell Property Solutions, was all about coming up with creative solutions to help people with their real estate needs. Having once owned a bank and title company, I knew there were legal ways to help minimize, or even eliminate, the judgments and second mortgage. Here was my win-win solution:

After reviewing their judgments, I knew I could get the $65K of total judgments eliminated for $5K (a legal process that would take sixty days), saving them $60K, which would go right to their bottom line. I also saw their second mortgage was owned privately, and I thought I could get the owner of the loan to take the principle only—forgoing the back interest, saving the property owners another $15K. I said, "If I can do that, would you agree to give me a discount of $25K off my purchase price," which is my additional cost, "to properly fix the water issues and structural damage?" They agreed, as did I.

The last issue we needed to address was the tax auction, which was ten days away. I told them that I would lay out the money now to save the house and pay the back taxes. We had the attorneys draft the agreement for the advancement, and we saved their house. We successfully got the judgments removed; it cost them $7K—not $5K—and the second mortgage waived all back payments, so long as they could receive their principle.

Water, Mold, and Structure

(how we dealt with the issues and solved the problem by focusing on the solution)

Before hiring any specialists, Easy Sell Property Solutions reviews the issues. If we feel a necessity for a more experienced person to review the situation, we then hire engineers and specialists. In the case of Elm Street, we hired a structural engineer (a foundation expert), as well as a geologist. Both of them gave incredible insights as to what needed to be done in order to correct the issue.

The structural engineer explained that in order to correct the sinking foundation and bulging foundation wall, we needed to jack up the house itself, underpin the foundation, and reinstall a new foundation wall. Based on the structural engineer's inspection, once the water issues were taken care of, along with the mold, we could then jack up the house for foundation work. The geologist gave us direction as to how to implement a French drain system to remove all water from within the home before raising it up.

A French drain is a trench filled with gravel or rock, or containing a perforated pipe that redirects surface water and groundwater away from an area (*see also:* weeping tile, blind drain, rubble drain, rock drain, drain tile, perimeter drain, land drain, French ditch, subsurface drain, subsoil drain, or agricultural drain). These sometimes involve perforated hollow pipes placed along the bottom of the trench to quickly vent water that seeps down through the upper gravel.

French drains are primarily used to prevent ground and surface water from penetrating or damaging building foundations. Another possible use is to distribute water, such as a septic drain field at the outlet of a typical septic-tank sewage treatment system. French drains are also used behind retaining walls to relieve ground-water pressure. This solution (a) allowed the basement to remain dry and mold free, and (b) made the home easy to sell by showing we had redeveloped the proper way. For these reasons, it was the only logical decision to make; the other option would have been knocking the house down and building a home without a basement—which was unnecessary. The new owners, after we redeveloped, loved the home and the fact that we chose to do this the proper way.

So, we redeveloped the home, the right way. First, the home was gutted down to the studs. We needed to get the water issue under control, so we fixed the foundation and installed the French drain system. Next, we had the mold remediation team come in full white suits to spray and scrub every inch of the home. After that, they closed off the house in a huge, commercial-sized, air-mold remediation system, which needed to run for five days. At the end of the five days, we retested the air quality and surfaces. It's only when the tests come back with a pass, along with a mold-remediation certificate that you are able to start redeveloping the home with insulation and drywall. Mold is serious. Many redevelopers out there do not remediate it the proper way; some just spray bleach on the walls thinking that kills it. Wrong! You need to remediate mold the proper way, which is by-no-means cheap, but it's the right way to do it.

We hired a company who specialized in mold remediation. They are licensed and insured for this process. Our in-house project manager handled the coordination of this work. After the five days for testing, remediating took another eleven. From beginning to end, when we received the certificate, it took a little over two weeks; but we were initially told the mold count was extremely high—toxic, in fact. We followed their recommendations to cure the issue the right way. The right way is almost always the most expensive option; but *when you are in the field of redeveloping homes, you need to do it in a certain way.*

We went through the process, the costs, and the guarantees. And what we also did was hire a separate company who does the testing to ensure that the remediation company was doing the proper job; personally, I've come to believe it's always good to have checks and balances. By hiring an outside testing company, we held the remediation company to a higher standard. Both air and surface samples were taken at the end, which were sent to a lab. The lab then sent the results back to the company who had done the testing.

As per the structural engineer's advice, once the water issues were addressed, we found ourselves a licensed contractor specializing in foundations, and the engineer signed off on it. This company secured the foundation, jacked up the house, built a new foundation wall, and then, they finished everything by underpinning the foundation. While the process was costly, overall, it was extremely smooth.

Lessons Learned:

1. Regardless of how bad a situation seems at first, if you think creatively, you can always come up with alternative solutions.

   - Most investors would have given up on this opportunity after they had all the info about the deal.

   - Because of our background in banking and title, we were able to creatively fix the problem.

2. *Always* thoroughly inspect the properties upfront, even if you are short on time.

   - Go through the proper due diligence steps.

3. Don't overthink things—*take action.*

Problems:

1. Property had water issues and mold.

2. Property foundation was sinking.

3. Sellers thought they had equity

   - But they had multiple judgments

   - and a second mortgage

Solutions:

1. We had the water issues and foundation issue reviewed.

2. We decided to put in a French drain system and remediate the mold.

   - We got a mold certificate showing the house was free and clear of mold and that the water problem was rectified.

3. We also consulted with a foundation expert.

   - The solution was to jack up the rear part of the house and redo the foundation.

4. We went to court and used a legal technique which allowed us to eliminate the $65k of judgments—the cost was only $7k.

5. We negotiated the back interest to zero—paying off the private lender principle only.

Winners in the End

Everyone walked away happy. Final result—the sellers were able to sell a nonsalable house. We successfully removed the judgments and minimized the second mortgage payoff—and received a $25k discount off the sales price due to the condition of the property. We did everything properly, abiding by the recommendations of every expert needed to get this property repaired and remediated. Overall, it was a win-win for all parties. After fixing everything, we left the deal with a profit, and the two sellers were able to restart their lives separately with some cash in hand. Finally, the new buyers got a structurally sound, 100 percent-remodeled home that passed all inspections and was done to code. All in all, everyone won.

If you have a house anywhere in New York and would like to see how our unique selling solution, "The Easy Way Out," can help you sell your home in the fastest, easiest, most hassle-free manner—and close on a date of your choosing, guaranteed—call us at 631-400-EASY(3279) or fill out our online inquiry at EASYSELL411.com. Also be sure to listen to us on 103.9 LI News Radio every Saturday at 12–12:30 p.m. or listen online at linewsradio.com.

OVERCONFIDENT NEWBIES

By
Greg Zytkowski & Russell Taylor

Columbus

Our names are Greg Zytkowski and Russell Taylor. We are Franklin Real Estate Partners, and we're from Columbus, Ohio. We're business partners but we're also best friends, too. We met back in the fall of 1996 at Ohio State University—Go Buckeyes!

We've been working together in various companies and shops since 2003. We formed Franklin Real Estate Partners in 2012 to start buying rental properties and rehabbing homes. We started off wanting to learn as much as possible about real estate. We came across a book, which many people are surely familiar with, *Rich Dad Poor Dad*, by Robert Kiyosaki; it explores the many benefits of being a business owner, creating passive income, and using real estate to push ahead and accomplish those goals. Kiyosaki's work really spoke to us.

Since both of us are children of educators, it was just very natural for us to seek out education, to find people who were successful in doing things, and then model ourselves after them so we could achieve those goals. We signed up for a real estate mentoring program and dove right in, hoping to become real estate entrepreneurs. We spent a good year learning all about it before we actually started doing deals. Not only did we spend the full year working full-time and learning about it, we also spent a whole lot of money on the education that came along with it. Some of it was essential. Maybe some of it—looking back on it—we didn't need, but it was good, because it kept us accountable to ourselves and each other to do the tremendous amount of work it takes to learn all the moving parts of real estate transactions and how all these parts interact with each other.

Fast-forward to now and we are buying as many houses per month as we did in our whole first and second years combined. We truly enjoy working with people and looking for ways to help people solve the many different and unique problems that come attached with real estate. Our company motto is "Building a Tradition of Trust," and we try to live up to that in everything we do. There have been so many people we have helped over the years get out of stressful and negative situations that couldn't have been helped by traditional routes of selling properties (i.e. using a real estate agent). We could probably write a book on the crazy situations we have encountered, but for now we will stick to one in particular and tell you what we did wrong and what we learned from it.

Blue Bell Drive

(our second house)

After our first year of education, we finally decided to jump in and buy a property. We bought a house that we were planning on holding as a rental, but we ended up selling it instead. With this house, we sort of stumbled into a solution that worked for both us and the seller of the property. We ended up rehabbing and selling to make a little bit of money. The seller was so happy we got them out of their situation that they came to the open house just to congratulate and thank us again. We thought, "Well that was easy; we are experts now." So we went out to look for another one.

We came in contact with a couple facing a tax foreclosure situation on their house. They were really up against it; their taxes were due, and they did not have the money to pay. Their home needed some repairs, and they couldn't afford to pay for them to get the house to a condition to sell and break even. Also, they didn't have the time to put the house on the market and wait for months until it sold—if it sold at all. We worked closely with them to construct an offer that would bring their taxes current, halt the foreclosure, and then give them some money on top to be able to move.

As it happened, our offer came at the right time and really helped them out. They were able to save what they could out of the house and then, afford to move to Georgia and buy a new place without having their credit ruined by foreclosure. They were very grateful and excited, once they realized that we actually did what we said we were going to do.

Many people think that to get a deal on a house you need to be nefarious (doing something underhanded, word of the day . . .), as if you're stealing a property from somebody. In this situation, it truly was a win-win. They didn't have many choices, and we were able to act sooner rather than later; this also helped us get the property. We made them the offer, and the offer got accepted.

Looking back on things, we realize this is where our first challenge came into play: the due diligence phase, which is fancy talk for doing research on what a house should be worth, once fixed up, and what it would cost in rehab to get it there. People can get into trouble in this area by either doing all this research themselves, while not truly understanding all that factors into coming up with values, or asking the wrong people for advice. You would be amazed by how many real estate agents actually don't have the slightest idea about any of this, yet will be more than happy to provide you with an answer anyway!

There is also the question of what repairs are really needed. Where do you get the most "bang for your buck"? The answer is simple: kitchens and bathrooms—right? That's somewhat right; but within those two rooms lie multiple pitfalls and thousands of dollars that can be misspent. What level do you need to fix these rooms up to? Do you need granite countertops? How about 30-inch cabinets vs. 42 inches? Should you keep the current layout, or completely gut everything and start over? The answer? It depends.

For the house on Blue Bell Drive, we had developed a rough budget for our construction rehab, and had an idea of what the house would be worth after it was fixed up. We decided to go for it, so we borrowed the money from a hard money lender (a specialized lender for rehab projects, typically expensive) and bought the house. Almost immediately after we began construction, we started to come up with different values for how much we thought the house would sell. We started to think it was worth more than we initially thought.

We were looking at all the houses that sold in the area and comparing them to our house. We had debates back and forth leading to a $35,000 swing in what we originally thought we could sell for, and almost every value in between. Looking back, we realize we weren't being objective; we were way too close to assess it clearly and way too emotionally involved. This can be a very dangerous thing when dealing with the valuation of houses.

One way this can lead to problems is when choosing what types of finishes to install. For instance, at a higher price point, houses need certain upgrades like granite countertops over the less expensive alternative. Here is a common pitfall: you think your house is going to be worth more than it ever could be (every neighborhood has a price ceiling), so you start adding more expensive finishes, thinking it will make the house sell for more. Truth is, there are many houses in which you could install gold-plated faucets with imported Italian marble (there are people who will happily sell you these items), and it still won't raise the value of the house over the ceiling of the neighborhood.

So, if you think your house will sell for more, you start spending more on things like granite and hand-scraped hardwood floors. This can lead you down a path of over-improving a house. We've actually seen people spend more on rehab than the house is worth!

We had an interior designer help us out, and our contractor had a stager/designer, as well. Everybody involved had input on what we needed to do, or what we shouldn't do to make the house beautiful. "There were too many cooks in the kitchen," is the analogy, and that's exactly what was going on for us.

Another problem we encountered was suffering from delusions of grandeur. We watched all the different flipping programs on TV. We saw the cool stuff people were doing, so we said, "Let's open up the kitchen walls so the floor plan's more open. We can gut and remodel the master bathroom and redo the hallway bathroom," even though it was in really good shape and maybe only needed a mirror and some painting; but we said, "No, we'll redo flooring and fixtures and vanity and everything." We added granite and hand-scraped hardwood floors, which we still do to this day, but only when it's called for.

We should've been asking ourselves, "Hey, are the interior doors good enough to just fix one of them and paint the rest?" However, we said, "Nope, if we're going to switch one, let's switch them all out." And in an average 1,800-square-foot, four-bedroom, two-and-a-half bath house, there can be fifteen to twenty doors. These are the types of decisions that, when you get further down the road and realize where to spend your money, you may or may not do something like that. It all depends on what is happening in the neighborhood and market conditions.

Someone wanting to put their house on the market needs to understand that there might be a small number of improvements that should be made; however, it's really tough to know where to spend your money, and it's really tough to not overspend. The reverse is also true. Some people think they can get a house to the top of the market with a quarter of what it would take to get there. They tend to figure that out about a quarter of the way into a renovation. These decisions and situations get especially tough when you're emotionally tied to a house.

All told, we spent about $20,000 over our original rehab budget. The sad thing about this is that none of it actually raised the value of the house because we spent it on the wrong things. Our delusions of grandeur and—*Just go ahead!*—over-improving a property were one thing; but the real mistake we made, the real nightmare was the misevaluation of the value of the home on the front-end, when we were doing our due diligence.

When we were first figuring out how much we thought the house was worth, we were saying, "Well that house over there sold for X dollars, so ours will sell for Y." We had no method or real life experience for how to systematically work these numbers, and we let our emotions take the wheel. We pretty much just based our numbers on a gut feeling (our primary strategy . . .). The other thing we didn't have any knowledge of was what was going on in the market at the time and the many quiet factors that were affecting the value of our house (some of them are completely invisible to the average person who doesn't live and breathe real estate).

What we know now is that coming up with values is both a science and an art. There is a mix of systematically comparing the numbers and also going with a gut feeling, although it really helps to have experience before you place too much trust in this. In reality, none of our repairs or work on the property noticeably changed the values. We could've put in an additional $30K or $40K. Honestly, sky's the limit on what you can spend on a house; but there's a ceiling on what you can sell it for and almost every neighborhood has a ceiling.

Our next mistake was thinking we knew how to navigate the waters of putting a house on the market and selling it. Now keep in mind, we did sell the house; but looking back, we realized how many mistakes we made and how much money those mistakes ended up costing us. The very first offer we received, which we thought was too low, ended up being the offer we came back to about six months later. Since we didn't have a better understanding of the process, had we hired a GOOD real estate agent from the beginning, they would have more than paid for themselves during the negotiation process and saved us months of stress.

The problem is there are a lot of real estate agents out there, and maybe 10 percent are the super-seasoned, phenomenal agents you should hire. The other 90 percent don't know what they are doing and will cost you time and way more money. Also, many people have someone in the family or a close friend who is an agent, so it is expected that they are to be hired—this can be a HUGE mistake.

Here are just a few of the very important questions that arose in our process and also some questions for someone who wants to sell their house to consider, all of which we didn't really know the answers to when we started out and most of which cost us money:

- Do I need to rehab areas of my house? If so, what areas?
- How much should I spend?
- Should I do the work myself or hire someone?
- If I do it myself, how long will it take to finish and will I finish?
- How much should I list my house for?
- If I realize I've priced it too high, what do I do next?
- How long do I keep it at that price before considering a price cut, and how much?
- How fast are properties moving in my market and also in my immediate area?
- At what length of time will my property develop a stigma for being on the market too long?
- How many people are going to come through my house before I get an offer?
- How do I handle showings?
- How many months will this take?
- Someone has made an offer; how do I know if it's legit?
- What happens if we fall out of contract?
- How many times can we fall out of contract before my property develops a stigma?
- Why does the buyer's bank keep asking for extensions?
- What title company should I use?
- Who is a good real estate attorney?

- The buyer is asking for me to fix certain items, and it could cost me thousands; should I fix them or offer a credit?

The questions go on and on and can overwhelm quickly. A great real estate agent can guide you through this process, which can take many months and bring much stress.

Lessons Learned

1. Remove emotions when dealing with selling a home

2. You can spend a lot of time and money on fixing a house up and not improve the overall value.

3. Not understanding your market can cost you

4. Taking the first offer that makes sense and moving on can be more important than waiting for the best offer.

5. Sometimes accepting less money and moving quickly can far outweigh the stress and time it takes to get a higher price.

A great mentor of ours always says, "In real estate, you are either making money or getting an education." Truer words have never been spoken when we look back on our experience with Blue Bell. The bottom line is if you are planning on selling a house, consider either of the following: (a) find the best real estate agent in your area, expect to wait a lot longer for your payday, and pay them what they are worth, or (b) deal with folks like us and sell your house quickly and easily.

Should you come to a point where the quick and easy solution of selling your Columbus, OH house makes the most sense, please visit our website at www.frepartners.com to see what we can do for you, or reach out to us at (614) 468-5428, or via email at frepartners@gmail.com, or Greg@frepartners.com.

When you're ready, the authors of this book came together to create just for you a 15-point checklist (with pictures) to help maximize your potential and profit in selling your house on your own. You can download a complimentary copy of, **"15 Must-Do Steps to Successfully Selling Your House On Your Own"**, at NoAgentNeeded.com

MISCOMMUNICATION, FUMIGATION AND RESTORATION, OH MY!

By
Jeff Garner

I'm a self-made man in a way. I grew up with my father and my grandparents; I bounced back and forth until my grandparents passed away when I was ten. I never had a full-time mom, as she moved to Texas when I was eleven months old, but I have a stepmom who filled the role as best she could. I went to eleven schools and never graduated; I was too busy following in the family footsteps, drinking and partying, and school only got in the way.

When I was twenty-three, I was a mess: an alcoholic with a drug problem. I had been this way for about five years and realized I would either stop or die or end up in prison. So, I focused on sobriety and recovery and learned how to live differently. I hit an emotional bottom. I wanted a family, success in business, and even more, peace and serenity. I knew I wasn't powerful enough to stop on my own, so I needed to find a power greater than myself, whom I choose to call God. I've spent the last nineteen years working on my spirituality (not religion), and helping others. I share this part of me because I believe it's made me who I am as a father, friend, and businessman. I like to say I've never been educated enough to know what I'm *not* supposed to be able to do—LOL—so, if I wanted to do or have something, I did whatever it took to get there. There's no such thing as a roadblock.

I feel like having lived through that point in my life plays a big part in who I am today, and I wouldn't change it. Immediately after getting sober, I got my real estate license. I was nervous that I wouldn't be any good; but my father owned a real estate company, and I didn't have a high school diploma, so what else would I do? Turned out, I was a success; I ended up selling hundreds of homes in the first few years, mainly to investors. These particular deals turned out to be my niche; I had an eagle's eye in finding them, and I was great at evaluating property.

After the first three years, I realized I needed to be on the other side of the closing table— the buyer and seller side, not the agent side. I started buying for myself, rehabbing, and selling. I grew my number of agent sales, and when I was doing about twelve rehabs a year in 2010, I then committed myself to being a full-time investor; I loved investing. During all of this, I realized that 90–95 percent of the market can list with a real estate agent because they have money, time, and resources; but 5–10 percent cannot list because they have distressed real estate or a distressed life situation. This 5–10 percent is underserved, and they often end up in foreclosure or giving their property away; so I began building my real estate business around serving them, marketing directly to sellers in distressed situations.

I built my business around helping people, not just buying ugly homes. My company understands that, in most situations, money is only a small part of the problem. We try to offer whatever our clients need to improve their lives, and buy their property at a fair cash price. We've become one of the largest local, home-buying companies in the St. Louis metro area. All of our clients give us testimonials after closing; mostly, their transactions with us have improved their lives.

A Burnt Home

My office received a call from a couple who had a fire in their home. They wanted to move on and sell the house as is. It sounded like a smaller fire, but nonetheless, they had received enough from the bank to pay off their loan, plus some. It seemed like they were reasonable about their asking price, so I met with them to evaluate the repairs and give them a cash offer.

When I walked up to the house, I could see that the windows were boarded up in the front, but the exterior of the house was brick and it looked very clean; it appeared still in really good shape. I could tell the fire didn't do too much damage to the structure or the roof, nor did the roof have any holes. Generally, a house catching fire can be a scary ordeal because the flames can burn into the rafters, causing structural damage, or into the joists under the floor; this house had a basement, and it was, in fact, burnt through the joists. Regardless, inspection of joists, rafters, and the like is the key to evaluating a house to assess how badly a fire may have damaged the structure.

So I felt pretty optimistic walking up to the house. A lot of times, we pass on houses that have been burnt because they're almost always teardowns. I went into the house. The sellers lead me through the front door, and we walked into the main living room, which was in the center. To the right, I could see that there was heat and smoke damage on the main level. All the drywall was bubbled, the paint was melted off, and it was all black. As I looked from there to the ceiling, I could see the black fading to the original white of the drywall. I was optimistic because I could see there was only heat damage on the main level from the fire below, so the flames didn't actually make it through the floor above the main level.

Everything I saw was an indication to me that there was a really good chance it was structurally sound; the fire was more of a cosmetic burn. The floor had a little charring, and I could tell the flames had been directly beneath it. Next, we did a quick walk through the main level, down the hallway, and we looked in the bathroom and three bedrooms, where there was virtually no damage whatsoever; the walls were still white from the original paint. I was still confident the fire really had been contained to the main level and that the damage was primarily in the living room.

While the sellers were showing me everything, I instantly saw a way to make the house a little more appealing. I could take down the center wall that separated both the kitchen and dining room from the living room and entry, making it one big room, giving it more of an open feel. So, I kind of noted that in my head. I went downstairs where the fire had been. When I looked at the ceiling from there, I could see there was some charring on the joists, but only two or three spots that we would need to replace. At that point, I knew we wouldn't even need to replace those joists; we could sister another joist next to each, strengthening the weak spots by providing the support of two joists along those areas, instead of one.

These joists ran from one side of the basement to the other, big two-by-sixes, and they ran about every twelve inches to hold up the upstairs level. Along different areas in the basement, there were posts in the concrete that supported the joists. The concrete foundation was fine, and I really felt like we could just run some extra joists along the ones that were burnt, actually giving it greater stability.

We previously found the needed fumigation chemical (basically a superpowered Microban that kills bacteria and things that create odor) from a fire restoration company, which could clean all the soot and charring off the whole house, as well as eliminate the smell. I knew I could get a hold of this chemical, but that stuff's expensive, as is hiring a fire restoration company to come in and restore the home for you. Hiring a company would cost around $10K, but it would cost me only $1000 to just buy the chemical for myself. All these factors were going through my mind as to why I should take on this rehab.

I knew I could gut that basement area because it had only a little bit of finishing. It had a big closet and some paneling on the walls, and there were frames. I thought I would tear all that out, remove the burnt wood, fix the joists, and then fumigate and clean all the soot and fire damage out of the house. And I thought I'd paint the walls and floor, and nobody would ever know the fire had happened. I could easily handle the repairs of scraping the bubbled paint off the walls on the main level, and then I could tear that wall down to have a big, open room, repaint, and all the fire damage would be gone. The house would be a reasonably quick and easy rehab so I was excited. The couple could then file an insurance claim and receive enough money to pay off the mortgage with $26K left over. From my evaluation of the property, I determined the house needed $25K in repairs, and that the after-repair value (ARV) would be $85K.

The problem was that the city wouldn't give them the overage from paying off the mortgage until they rehabbed the property. So my company would need to buy the property and rehab the house; then, not only would we be able to sell it, but also the city would release the $26K they were holding to ensure the work was done. The couple told me they wanted to move on, getting as much as they could now, and leave the $26K to us; I was surprised, but excited. We wrote the contract for $9K and set it to close in a week with the expectation we would receive the $26K of overage at the end.

So our impression was that the couple had their house paid off and just wanted to move ASAP with some money in their pocket, as so often is the case. The day before closing, the seller informed us that not only would they not let us have the $26K, they were under the impression that we would buy the house for $9K, give them their overage ($26K) at closing, and then collect from the city when the rehab was done. This was definitely not the deal I made, but the seller said they were backing out if we didn't do it that way.

I was so close to closing and it was an amazing deal before, but I decided it would still be worth doing even though I wouldn't get the extra money at the end of the rehab. Still, I wasn't going to float that overage at closing. So in an effort to create a win-win, I proposed that we would buy it for $9K, and let them collect the money at the end of the rehab, but we would not give them their overage at closing. It was this or nothing. This was the only way to achieve a win-win.

After they agreed, we paid the $9K, closed, and began the renovation. During the rehab, we ran across some new challenges. The city was extra tough on us because there had been a fire; they made us tear out duct work and replace the HVAC (heating and air-conditioning) systems, which seemed to be in great shape. We had to do unnecessary electrical and some carpentry. We also needed to use the special chemicals, which are very expensive, in order to get the smell out of the house. So many of these extra items were unexpected and cost me an additional $10K. That hurt, as the day before closing, I'd already lost $36K in this property—not to mention, I lost valuable time due to delays, waiting for the city to approve our work.

Up to this point, these were our two main mistakes:

1. Not putting the overage money in writing.

    -   Unfortunately, people lie, or at least, there can be miscommunication and/or details missed. They had me over the barrel, days before closing, and I had nothing about it in writing.

    -   I chose to give them the benefit of the doubt; I saw this as a communication disagreement.

2. Not having a fire restoration expert help with the repair evaluation.

    -   This would have determined a more accurate rehab number.

The Rehab

It was about halfway through the renovation when we realized that all the duct work would need to be taken out because we couldn't remove the smell of the soot and the smoke. The ducts begin on top of the furnace in the basement, and each duct ends after running between the joists (that's where a hole's been cut in the floor for a vent), and then, it all just branches off from that furnace into every room. This wasn't a fun thing to replace; it was also expensive, and we hadn't accounted for it. After replacing the ducts, we then discovered that the furnace (although it was in perfect condition and only a few years old) would need to be replaced, as well, due to the smell. HVAC systems are really easy to install; it just involves buying a piece of equipment when your duct work's good to go, but that wasn't the case for us.

And then, some of the electrical system was charred, which I hadn't been aware of, and to top that off, there were some necessary electrical updates. Since I was doing an extensive renovation, the city threw that in, basically saying, "Well, since you're at it . . . " We pulled the entire electrical system out, and in some areas, it was difficult.

When you wire a house while it's being made, there's no drywall, so you're just running wires through the house to each room and back to the panel. But when wiring a closed-up house (replacing wires two to three decades down the line), you need to carefully remove it without breaking the drywall. Once all of the wires are removed, then you need to run new wires behind the drywall, fish it downstairs, do all the finishings, and then finally, run it all the way back to the panel. This type of detailed work requires a specific type of experience in a licensed electrician, typically accompanied by three times the expense—oh boy, more money there as well.

For application of the fumigation chemical, you usually hire a fire and restoration company. Because they have all the training and they generally work with insurance companies, they get higher rates, and they really value their time. Typical rehabbers can't afford to hire a restoration company, but you can get a hold of the chemical on your own, and you can do the work yourself just as efficiently. We did it for less than $1,000. These insights set our company apart from the competition, and it's a reason we can pay more than anyone else.

The Overall Problems:

1. The sellers misinterpreted our deal.
2. We needed to use an expensive fumigation chemical.
3. We needed to replace the HVAC system.

4. The electrical system required updates beyond the fire damage.

Our solution:

1. I negotiated the sale to $9K, with the overage money to be paid at closing, and still bought the house.

2. I saved 50 percent on the fire treatment by doing it ourselves.

3. I used a refurbished HVAC system from another property in my portfolio to satisfy the city; that was another $3,000 saved.

4. We hired a specialized electrician to properly complete the work and comply with the city's demands.

All the extra work added an additional month getting it onto the market. I listed the property on the Multiple Listing Service (MLS) myself, as well as with a real estate agent, asking a reasonable price, at which we knew it would sell. Luckily, it sold fast enough to make up for lost time and the additional expense. The final result was that a first-time home buyer got an amazing new home; the original sellers received their money, enabling them to move on with their lives; and I was decently compensated. Win-win-win!

If you'd like to talk to us about how to sell your house in the greater St. Louis metro area as is, close fast, and avoid agent commissions, give us a call at 314-333-5555. You can also visit us at www.startingpointRE.com.

OVERGROWN IN PLEASANT GROVE

Problems Big and Small in Birmingham, AL

By
Jason Hollon

I've lived in my adopted home of Alabama for nearly twenty-five years, specifically residing in Birmingham for most of that time. My lovely wife, Robin, and I got married in 2006, and we are now raising our two beautiful daughters in Birmingham, along with a fluffy pet or two. My interest in real estate started at a young age, when I learned of a friend's uncle who was in the rental house business. Though I was really intrigued by that, I never did much to act on my interest until later in life. In the meantime, I worked as a Certified Public Accountant (CPA), finance professional, and management consultant.

After eventually making a foray into the rental housing business, I linked up with a local expert in Birmingham real estate who became my mentor and coach. He really got me started in additional aspects of the real estate business, and I soon became a full-time investor, creating value throughout the community. Since then, I have completed hundreds of transactions, and have consulted with thousands of other sellers, beyond that, to help find solutions for their particular situations.

My own real estate company, Brighter Day Homes, was started in 2010, and we haven't looked back since. We are completing transactions with dozens of sellers each and every year , and we continue to grow. We've experienced many different types of seller situations: old houses, new houses, houses in great shape, houses in bad shape, small houses, big houses, and just about everything in between.

Overgrown in Pleasant Grove

Pleasant Grove is a nice suburb outside of Birmingham. In 2011, much of the city was devastated by a large tornado that came through the area, and a house brought to my attention was one of those damaged homes. It was an inherited and unwanted vacant property. The property was a veritable forest of overgrown bamboo, trees, and bushes—it was nearly impossible to walk around, the vegetation was so thick. The house itself was still standing and structurally sound, so at least, there was something to work with.

The owner, someone with whom I already had a relationship, approached me about buying the house. Though the owner was another experienced real estate investor, they weren't set up to do the larger "hairy" rehabs the way we were at Brighter Day Homes. This seller was more of a part-time investor; whereas, I was doing rehabs full-time on a daily basis.

The owner was not a distressed seller. In fact, we often work with far more distressed properties, as opposed to distressed sellers; although, of course, we work with both. Typically, sellers have multiple options at their disposal, but they simply don't want to fool with the hassles of making repairs and dealing with contractors, inspectors, appraisers, and real estate agents, as well as keeping the house constantly clean for picky "looky-loo" buyers trudging through the home during showings.

The house in Pleasant Grove was a unique situation, where the needed repairs were so extensive that there really wasn't a way for us to buy it at a price that made any business sense for both parties involved. After all, any transaction needs to work for both the seller and the buyer. In other words, with a conventional type of cash purchase, there was very little incentive for them to sell it to us for nothing.

So we came up with a solution where I bought a half-interest in the house for a nominal fee. This was a very unique deal using what is called a "Tenants In Common" (TIC) interest, and we agreed to split everything on the back end, after all the costs were considered. For my part of the bargain, I agreed to do all the work to manage the property, clear the overgrown forest swallowing the house, bring the house back to a livable condition, and completely remodel it. This TIC arrangement isn't something I'd normally do, but it was a creative solution to this specific problem.

Going through with a TIC was a good choice for this project because I already knew and had a relationship with the owner. A TIC is just a way for different parties to hold a partial interest in a property. If you ever use this method, it's important to be sure the other person is someone you can trust.

Rehab began with some major landscaping work. This wasn't a project for the friendly neighborhood lawn service to take care of. It required a commercial landscaping company to bring in heavy equipment to get the job done. There were some drastic "before-and-after" pictures taken from the same standpoint, where you couldn't even see the house at all in the before shot!

The interior of the house was completely gutted. The seller previously had a bad contractor, who basically quit midway and—I would imagine—ran off with the money, as well. So we were working with a complete shell of a house, requiring a total rehab from the ground up. We had to redesign both the kitchen and bath layouts from scratch, which ended up being pretty nice as we could design it in the best way possible.

We worked closely with the city inspector, the mayor, and with the utility companies. We worked with the contractors and coordinated the detailed scope of work to be done. To this day, it is one of the largest rehabs in our portfolio. After completing everything, we made the arrangements to list the house on the Multiple Listing Service (MLS). The house sold quickly to a proud homeowner, who now has a beautiful new home.

Putting It All Together

The Pleasant Grove house was brought back not just to livability, but up to modern design standards. As with all rehabs, the neighbors loved to see the house come back to life. The property had long been an eyesore for the neighborhood as well as the entirety of Pleasant Grove —even the mayor often stopped by during rehab to express his gratitude and check on our progress. A new certificate of occupancy was issued from the city inspector, with whom we maintained a relationship during the whole process. All together, we installed a new kitchen, new bathrooms, new flooring, paint and Sheetrock, electrical and plumbing updates, doors and windows, a new garage door, new heating and air systems, and a new roof, as well as completely overhauled the landscaping.

A house in this condition is a big job, but not the end of the world. Our solution was fairly simple:

A. Buy the house in a nonconventional manner in order to structure a transaction that works for both us and the seller.

B. Tightly manage the rehab process to create a successful transaction for both parties.

There is a solution to most real estate problems, no matter the condition, location, size, shape, or price range of the house. To avoid setbacks, also be aware of potential issues with your title, and consider ordering a preliminary title search if you are concerned about it. Unexpected title flaws are not uncommon, and we often assist sellers in working with a title company to get such matters cleared up.

Don't despair about needed repairs or junk in the house—we've seen it all and deal with it every day—and if you decide to do your own repairs and updates, remember that it needs to be done by licensed professionals. Be sure that your updates conform to the desires of buyers in today's marketplace. *And do your homework before any repairs and updates!* It is very easy to overspend on unnecessary improvements, overlook other recommended improvements, and of course, get ripped off by a bad contractor.

The Best Option for You the Seller

If none of that seems too scary, you can always handle the work yourself. You will need to familiarize yourself with both what work needs to be done and what work should not be done. I find that it is very easy to over-improve a house and spend too much. Take a page from the previous owners of Overgrown in Pleasant Grove: you need to be very wary of bad contractors. It's just an endemic issue in the industry. Even for someone who's in the business day-to-day like us, dealing with contractors is a continual problem. You need to ensure you're using licensed professionals who pull permits, and that your updates are what today's marketplace desires so you're not doing too much or things that are already considered out of date by the current discerning home buyers.

In certain circumstances, Brighter Day Homes is happy to refer people to real estate agents whom we know and trust. Despite the theme of this book, there are circumstances where it is perfectly fine to list your house on the Multiple Listing Service using a real estate agent. If the below set of qualities sounds like you, then we are happy to refer you to a real estate agent:

- If your house is in fantastic shape and shows well
- If you have plenty of time (at least several months)
- If you don't mind the hassles of showing the property, which entail constantly keeping the house clean and ready for potential buyers to stream through
- If you're comfortable paying the holding costs for the property for at least six months, such as:
  - Mortgage payments
  - Insurance payments
  - Property taxes

- ○ Utilities
- ○ Homeowners' fees
- ○ Lawn and landscape maintenance
- ○ Regular maintenance and repairs on the house itself

Real estate agents are not equally talented, and we have deep industry contacts to guide you appropriately. We try to take more of a consulting approach and give people a sense of what might be their best option—whether it is a solution we can provide, or whether someone else (such as a real estate agent) would prove a more efficient fit. We tend to believe in karma, and that what goes around comes around. We find that sellers appreciate the honesty, and because of that approach, we tend to get consistent business from referrals and word-of-mouth.

Should the need arise where you'd like our help, a second set of experienced eyes and ears, a fast and easy sale of your property without additional costs or headaches, or just a sounding board for your ideas, feel free to contact us at 205-390-1050 or find us online at www.WeBuyBham.com.

When you're ready, the authors of this book came together to create just for you a 15-point checklist (with pictures) to help maximize your potential and profit in selling your house on your own. You can download a complimentary copy of, **"15 Must-Do Steps to Successfully Selling Your House On Your Own"**, at NoAgentNeeded.com

BARELY ESCAPING
THE JAWS OF
REAL ESTATE INVESTING

By
Parker Stiles

I was born and raised in Athens, Georgia, until moving to Kennesaw for college. I found the woman of my dreams my sophomore year, and we got married about six years later. Both of us are very outgoing and love pushing ourselves to be the best we can be. We currently own and operate Barrington Acquisitions; we purchase, renovate, and sell/hold both single- and multi-family properties around Atlanta, Georgia and Charleston, South Carolina. This occupation brings with it much stress and frustration at times; but those times always seem to be twice as rewarding once your past the finish line. We love doing what we do, and enjoy helping people handle their real estate-related situations.

Some of my interests aside from work include: hunting, spending time at the lake, traveling, wakeboarding, working out, snow skiing, and mountain biking!

Wilderness Way

One property I remember that was particularly stressful and frustrating was a house we handled on Wilderness Way, back around January 2016. It's a crazy story, and a long one, even just getting to the contract phase of the deal. It all started when a call came in from a nice lady who was in a not-so-nice situation.

A large family had grown up in this home with their parents, and before too long, had all moved away to different states to start their own families; however, the house was left uncared-for. The parents had passed ten years prior to the last child moving out, which had left the property vacant, ever since. We started jumping into how the deal would work, what my company does for people in similar situations, what her ownership role was, as well as the current condition of the property. Up to this point, it sounded like we would be able to help this nice lady and her siblings dispose of the outdated, dilapidated house.

When I went to visit the house, I was thrilled and skeptical at the same time. It was an old cedar-siding house, contemporary style, with all the crazy angles. It was just completely falling apart; I mean this place was *bad*. There were raccoons and birds living inside! They had chewed through the siding as well as the house wrap, insulation, and Sheetrock, taking over the master bedroom. We even found a large family of rats living underneath the bathtub!

I walked around to the back and found that a large deck had ripped off the side of the house and crumbled to the ground from the second story! As soon as I saw this, I knew there would be more work here than what appeared on the outside. In addition, I later found out that the city had actually placed an abatement hold on the property! In this case, that meant so many people had complained to the city that officials came out and flagged the property as unfit for human habitation, or that it possibly constitutes endangerment to the public health.

When I came back to discuss my newly found information, I found a couple of other issues. There were about seven family members who were owed their split of the proceeds—and it hadn't even gone through probate yet! So the person I was speaking with actually didn't yet have the legal authority to sell the house on her own. I was also told that a couple of investors previously tried buying the house, but were unsuccessful because of certain family members declining to sign their affidavit forms!

However, I got all the needed signatures by personally contacting all parties to see what problem I could solve for them. After about three months (working through the probate, paper-pushing among seven parties, and compromising with a couple of unwilling family members), I was able to purchase the four-bedroom, three-bath house for a great price. This house did need a ton of work, but our potential resale value was high enough to make it worth the risk.

Needless to say, I was excited to get started. I had been itching to renovate an older contemporary style home with crazy modern finishes, and now I had my chance. From day one the project started off fast; we probably had fifteen guys ripping the entire house down to the studs. We had plans to replace almost everything. As we cruised through the first stages of the renovation, there were some hiccups, but nothing too major; there were things like extra framing here and there, and some subfloor needing to be replaced, which had rotted from leaks in the roof and where the siding had come off the house in places.

There were tons of tennis ball-sized holes all around the house, where birds had just—for years and years—pecked right through, until they could build a nest inside. I had to give it to them: it looked like hard work! There were also wasp and hornet nests behind the cedar siding (let me just say how much I hate flying, stinging insects). When we were tearing down Sheetrock in the lower-level bonus room, we put a new can light into the ceiling and turned it on. After a couple of hours, it started getting hot, as lights do, but then this weird, black, kind-of-sticky stuff started dripping from the can light's seal—we thought it was the strangest thing.

We pulled the can light out and realized there was a beehive the size of a double-wide aluminum sink above the Sheetrock. When we installed the light, it heated the hive until the honey, or whatever was in there, started melting and dripping onto the floor. It was the craziest thing I've ever seen. We had to take the light out, cut a huge hole in the Sheetrock, and then, break away at this giant beehive, which had been developing through the years.

We pulled everything out. We filled up maybe three or four 40-yard dumpsters (an incredible amount of junk). After hauling those off, we began putting things back together. We installed new flooring throughout the house, and by flooring I mean, Italian porcelain tile planks over 1,800 square feet in all the common areas. We tiled the kitchen, bathrooms, living room, and even the stairs—all of it looked super cool!

Meanwhile, I picked up another house and hired the same contractor to do the renovation there as well. I paid him all the money up front for this other job, since it was smaller scale, and I had gained a trust level with him from our current and past projects. What I did not know is that my GC (general contractor) had recently run out of funds on Project One, and instead of telling me, had begun commingling the funds from Project Two, to use them on Project One. This created an accounting nightmare, once we found out, much later.

In addition, about 70 percent of the way through Project One, I was made aware by a third party that they did not believe my GC was licensed. From day one, he'd told me that he was, but I made the mistake of not asking for proof because of the trusting relationship we developed. When I looked him up, I discovered that he was, in fact, not licensed. I decided to call him and ask him again, and he directly lied to me.

I knew at this point that we had a real problem. I then began to think about permitting. We needed a full building permit from the city, as well as sub-permits for the scale of work needed. My GC told me he had been pulling permits since the beginning, as did all his subs (subcontractors). It also stated in my original bid that I paid $2,200 for permitting.

I immediately called down to the city and found that *no* permits had been pulled for Project One. This was a serious issue regarding resale and liability. At this point in time, we were listed on the open market and had just gone under contract with a buyer—for slightly over what we thought we could sell it for. The house looked amazing. We went over budget, but it was an enormous job. Actually, we accepted the buyer's offer while in Louisiana, at one of Matt Theriault's investor workshops. We were ecstatic because it was only on the market for around forty-eight hours, but we were very fearful of how the permitting issue would affect the sale.

Later that weekend, after returning to Georgia, we got a call from the buyer's agent, letting us know that their buyer was pulling out of their contract, immediately. "What is happening?" my wife and I asked each other. Literally, this was the perfect buyer, and we were dying for this project to be over. I soon found out why they pulled their offer.

When their property inspector went through the house, it was discovered that nearly half of the completed renovations were not done to Cobb County code. On top of that, their inspector found twelve plumbing leaks and numerous electrical issues, where the work was not done correctly. We later found out this happened because our GC had secretly been running dry on funds, which pushed him to hire low-end subcontractors to do the work for cheap. This is a very bad spot to be in. I felt like throwing up. Bad work could be fixed, but the permitting issue really scared me.

I was currently paying my lender about $1,500 per month in interest alone, on top of all the other holding costs involved. Additionally, in order for the house to sell, we needed to receive a Certificate of Occupancy (C.O.) from the city of Marietta—which meant we needed to pull a building permit and have all the necessary inspections completed (rough-in and finals). Well, there was one major problem with that: the rough-in inspections for plumbing, electrical, mechanical, and framing were supposed to happen *before* all the Sheetrock and tile was installed.

So, now it looked like we would be forced to rip out all our perfectly finished custom-tile showers, Italian porcelain flooring, and freshly painted Sheetrock. I hadn't eaten recently before hearing all of this; but if I had, whatever the meal, it might have ended up on the floor right about then.

Lessons Learned

A number of mistakes were made on this project, and I want to educate you on how to not make the same ones. Never pay your contractor in full, up front, for any project—no matter the size of the job or the relationship. Anything can happen. You need to keep your leverage because there are too many variables in this business to give that up. Trusting your contractor is very easy to do, once you develop a relationship with them; unfortunately, I learned that it's never smart to trust a contractor—no matter the circumstance.

Always ask to see proof of a contractor's license and insurance before hiring them. Some contractors are good with their words and use long complicated sounding sentences to trick you into thinking they are more experienced than they actually are. It is very easy for a contractor with a basic level of construction knowledge to talk circles around the average homeowner, or even some investors. Stand your ground and require seeing all documentation before starting any work or writing any checks. Also, if you're required to pull permits on your renovation, be sure to check that the permitting documents are in the permit box, and stuck in the front yard before starting any work. Also, make copies and save them in your files.

Estimating the costs of your rehab is another issue that often causes problems down the road. Most professional contractors can't even do this accurately. On this particular project, the original bid I received from my contractor was $91K. We ended up spending about $135K after all was said and done. As I complete more renovations, I add to my ongoing list of items that have a way of draining my wallet, so I can account for them in the beginning—instead of them stealing profits at the end.

One of the things we did originally—to mitigate our losses – was speak with an attorney. It's very hard to know what the right move to make is when there are so many rules in real estate and contracting. Our attorney, although not cheap, provided us with valuable insight into what we needed to do next. Confronting our GC and exploding with frustration toward him was definitely not the answer—no matter how much I wanted it to be. Since we had little to no leverage, we had to play our cards right if we wanted to get out of this alive.

I'm sure you have heard this a million times, but it's all about who you know. Also, it helps if the people you know also know many others. This was one thing that helped us save this deal. Our contractor's father actually had some connections with an engineering firm, who put us in contact with a gentleman who said he could guide us through the process of getting the sign-offs we needed—to get the city to approve the work, without tearing it all apart. However, we ran into another problem.

This new engineer thought we only needed sign-offs for structural and framing, which was his area of expertise. What we actually needed were sign-offs from an engineer for every side of the renovation—structural, mechanical, electrical, and plumbing. He was not comfortable doing this, so we were only 25 percent of the way there; however, he happened to know another engineer who was used to doing these types of sign-offs.

So, for a fee, our engineer recommended us to the other. We got an appointment set up at the earliest convenience, and paid about $750 for thirty minutes of the new-new engineer's time to do his thing. Now, to some, that may sound like a lot of money, but for the sign-offs that he gave us (without ripping anything down in the house), it was a miracle, and the steal of the century. After his stamped sign-offs were turned in to the city, we were able to schedule our final inspection with the code enforcer. I can't describe how lucky it was that this worked out the way it did.

This took two trips and around a thousand more dollars for certain repairs. Then we were finished! Finally, the C.O. was granted. It was like I had been in prison for ten years, just released back into the beautiful, free world.

Problem:

I trusted a contractor with too much responsibility, too soon.

Solution:

1. Always check proof of a GC's license and insurance.
2. Never start work without seeing the permit in person.
3. Don't give your GC more work than he is accustomed to handling.
4. Never pay your GC for all the work up front.
5. Be careful when having one GC do multiple projects for you at once to avoid commingling.

Shortly after getting the C.O., we re-listed the home and found a new buyer in the first week. We were able to close the deal in December— one year after we met the original owner. The fact that I learned as many lessons as I did with this sale, and still made some money, blows my mind to this day. It just goes to show, you have to buy right!

Never overpay for a deal, and never bring emotion into it. You need to stick to your numbers, or you will get beat up in this game. I've learned that (a) you can never trust a contractor, and (b) you always need to keep leverage on your side. Once you lose your leverage, you are playing with fire. Expect to get burned.

It has been said to learn from other people's mistakes for you won't be here long enough to make them all on your own. So, if there is anything that I or my team could possibly do to help you with your real estate ambitions or challenges in Atlanta, GA or Charleston, feel free to reach out via our website, at www.BarringtonHomeBuyers.com

THE HOMETOWN FLIP THAT ALMOST FLOPPED

The House That Nearly Ended My Real Estate Career

By
Jeremiah Johnson

Wichita

Having grown up in Clearwater, Kansas, I was surrounded by real estate as my mother was a broker. For perspective, I graduated high school with about sixty-three other students; it is a super-small town. After high school, I went to the University of Kansas, where I met my wife. After college, I landed a position in medical device sales and worked in that field for almost a decade. During that time, I had looked at the idea of real estate investing, but hadn't really gotten into it, despite reading tons of books on the subject. I was in an accident that shattered my left leg, and it was severe enough that the doctors talked about amputating my left foot. As a result of that accident, I couldn't perform the duties that I once did, walking around and/or standing all day, because of my injuries.

Consequently, the accident prevented me from walking for almost six months and left me fairly couch bound. I started listening to a ton of podcasts, as well as reading more material. I decided I would make a full-time career of real estate; I just didn't know how to get started. I enrolled myself in an education course hosted by a hard money lender in Denver, and that was where I met someone who later hired me to be an acquisition manager for their company. I became their top sales producer and ended up working with them for about three-and-a-half years.

After my time with them, I decided to go out and form my own company, Friendly Home Buyer Inc. We specialize in fix and flip, wholesale, and buy-and-hold investing. I have some pretty aggressive goals as I'm hoping to get into several new markets in the next three years, but so far, it's been a fun ride.

South Byers

The very first flip we did was a house on South Byers Street. It was a short sale that my brother brought to my attention—he's a Realtor® in Kansas. The previous owner of the house was behind on their payments and abandoned it, leaving it in pretty rough shape. It was built in the late 1800's. Due to my lack of experience with rehab projects, I didn't know that a house of that era brings a whole new set of problems, ones that newer houses don't usually come along with. The house was in Clearwater, the same small town I grew up in, and there was zero inventory of remodeled homes on the market.

It was a cute three-bedroom, one-bath home that had a detached two-car garage. It needed a full remodel, as it was left unlivable. When we made an offer, the property had an ARV (after-repair-value) around $115K–$120K; we made an offer in the $30K range, and we got it. We thought it was just a smoking deal. I worked on getting bids from general contractors; since this would be my first one, I really wanted to make sure I was squeezing as many dollars out of this project as I could, that I was running it as efficiently as possible.

Looking back, I made a few mistakes that could have been avoided. First off, I do not recommend anyone take on an 1800s-built house as a first, full remodel due to the many nuances involved. Second, my most fatal mistake was not hiring a professional general contractor when I'd never renovated a property before. I didn't know how to manage subcontractors well; I did everything by word-of-mouth and handshakes, and had very little control of costs or schedules, as a result.

I interviewed and got bids from a few different general contractors. They were all in the $25K–$35K range, which I thought seemed high for the material cost; I also thought I could get it done for less. I should have known that I didn't know what I was doing. In hindsight, I should have approached it differently. I decided I would do it in-house without a GC (general contractor), taking on a rehab of enormous scope. It appeared that subbing everything out, instead of hiring a professional GC, was the right choice because I'd read a few books . . .

When you sub things out, you're in charge of keeping everybody in order. The trade needs to go in a specific sequence from demolition to new construction. I had no idea of what I was doing, and I thought we could get it done for about $20K–$25K; that the project would go off without a hitch; and that it would add a good chunk to my 401(k). Little did I know, I was in for a painful dose of reality. We bought it at a good price, so I really thought we were on a solid foundation.

The property needed a full remodel, and it almost looked like a haunted house as we drove up to it. It'd been abandoned by the previous sellers, and for good reason. The cabinet doors were off their hinges, and there were holes in the walls—like the one where we could see from the dining room into the bathroom. The original foundation was built with stone blocks, which were everywhere, and there was about a six- to seven-foot crawl space or basement. To access this, we had to go down a really steep set of steps. The previous owner had kept his dogs down there and didn't clean up after them, so it smelled horrendous. The walls and ceiling had all started to cave in. The original owner had placed steel beams against the entire foundation, so we knew we needed to have that assessed.

When we walked upstairs into the living room, we could see the ceiling in the main living area was sagging, which we didn't think much of, at first. We thought there had been a roof leak and that the Sheetrock was coming down; but when we ended up taking it down to the studs while having the demolition done, we found out that it was an addition. What was thought to be a saggy ceiling was, in reality, a lack of reinforcement in the ceiling truss. Because there was no continuous supportive beam going across, the top floor was pushing down into the second floor, the main floor. The house was literally trying to cave in on itself. We had to build a makeshift frame to push the top floor back up with jacks until we could build a support for it. We didn't see this coming! Having had the structural engineer (while looking at that basement) tell us the house was fine, that we just needed to have the dirt regraded, we thought we'd be okay.

Something I haven't mentioned up to this point: I made this purchase with my own retirement funds so there'd be no interest expense. I thought that by purchasing it, I'd be fine because we could just pay for the remodel, pay the contractor to purchase all the material, and it would just be a quick thing—in and out in three months; but that just didn't happen. The $5K–$10K I thought I'd save by not hiring a general contractor proved to actually be four or five times more than that amount—in expenses.

After we got the house down to the studs, we did all the plumbing, then we brought in an electrician, and then we did the HVAC. We decided to start working on the Sheetrock. The sheet rocker delayed us a month-and-a half because we were a very small client to him. I didn't realize it at the front-end because he was a referral. This tends to happen a lot with contractors, which I didn't understand at the time, but they will take on too many jobs—and when you aren't their priority customer, then you just continually get bumped to the back of the line. When we were redoing the drywall (purchasing all the supplies as we went to Home Depot, everything added up quickly), our contractor began working on a big apartment complex. So we went days and days and days without anybody working on our property; but they were already paid half up front, so we were committed. We couldn't go to another contractor, without paying double, to have the Sheetrock done.

A big mistake was we didn't have any contracts with the contractors, or even anything in writing, requiring them to comply with a timeline. Another mistake I've figured out was that, with every subcontractor or contractor you have, you need to have an agreement that penalizes them if they aren't on schedule, on time, and on budget. If they go outside of those parameters, it needs to be approved in writing. In and of itself, this was a humongous learning experience: *If it's not in writing, it probably won't happen, and if it does, it won't be on budget or on time.* But going into it, I didn't know those things; I'd read about them but I thought we'd be fine, that people do the right thing, and that we could trust them to get things done.

We continued to hire what we thought was the least expensive option, and every time, it proved to be the most expensive. Eventually we got the Sheetrock completed, and then, all the windows were installed. We also had the roof installed, but after the roofer finished, we discovered he had cut corners. Yes, brand new shingles, but he didn't replace the pipe jacks, which are basically gaskets that go around all the pipes on your roof. Instead, he just roofed around it all and left the old ones. On the first big rainstorm, we had just finished painting, and the water came pouring through the ceiling onto our new paint, ceiling, and floors. We ended up having to re-repair the roof, and then, redo all the Sheetrock along the ceiling. It was just one thing after another.

We were seven months in—mind you, this was supposed to be a three-month project—and I was in a quasi-partnership with somebody else, where I was supplying the funds and he was managing the project. He had decided that this was more than he had signed up for, so I ended up doing what I should've done in the very beginning: I hired somebody to come in and finish the job from end to end, and cover all the details that I couldn't handle because I was out of state.

We finally got it wrapped up, and put it on the market. All in, by the time we sold this house, we were at 92 percent loan-to-value (LTV) total—not a good place to be when you are trying to sell. The house sold for $122K, which is exactly what we had forecasted; but by the time the work was finished—all the receipts and money tallied—we ended up paying four to five times more than we should have paid. We cleared about $6K on a $122K house in pretty close to a yearlong project. In the very beginning, had we just paid the purchase price of $30K and then hired the GC for another $30K, we would've cleared probably $35K on this project—and we would've been in and out in three months.

Lessons Learned

South Byers was a huge eye-opener for me. I learned that it's better to lean on the professionals who handle this stuff on a daily basis, as opposed to wearing every hat, trying to save money or make more money on a project, while acting outside your skill-set. If you take the route of wearing every hat, in turn, you really just increase your scope and your time. You will end up paying a lot more for the same service because you will usually need to bring someone else in to fix the errors.

Looking at the opportunity cost and the amount of time and money that was spent, I did not make anything on that property. I basically did it for free, but the education gained was invaluable. I mean, if you can do real estate wrong, I pretty much did it wrong on this first project. It really had the potential. Had I lost everything in my retirement account as a result, I might've been scared off, and then I would not have wanted to continue down this path; however, S. Byers was such a learning experience, that on my very next rehab, we turned it around in eight weeks—I let somebody else do the entire project, and it sold for over asking price in a weekend.

My first two houses were completely night and day in experience. Since then, I've flipped several more houses, and my company is currently doing a good amount of wholesaling— everything is taking off! Right away, S. Byers showed me you really need to rely on your team and surround yourself with excellent people. Don't try to do everything yourself because it's not the highest and best use of your ability. If you're not a general contractor, then you shouldn't try to be one. That's really what I learned from the house that almost ended my fledgling real estate career.

My main recommendation to any investor (new or seasoned, or even a homeowner) is this: *there's a reason why the craftspeople in their respective trades are the experts.* Do what you're good at because that's where you are the expert. When it comes to what you aren't good at, either find somebody you can partner with or hire that service out; the brain damage you will avoid and the value that you will create on that project—by putting your efforts and talents into things that you are really good at—will pay big dividends. The proof is in this S. Byers project.

1. It took me a year when, at most, it should've taken three months.

2. I went through so many different trades before hiring somebody who handled it well.

3. My next project only took eight weeks and sold over asking price.

Simply put, a professional who installs a light for $75 ends up costing less than someone who comes in and does a bad job, cutting into the wall, putting the light in, and leaving their tracks for $50. You end up having to pay the drywaller and painter to come back for an additional $100, putting you at $150 for what could have cost you $75. That being said, do your homework, check references, and look at prior work before you hire. My two cents: learn from my mistakes and focus more on *who* can do the dirty work for you rather than *how* you can do it yourself. You've likely got better things to do.

When you're ready to sell your Denver, CO or Wichita, KS house, or any house in between these two cities, there are several ways Friendly Home Buyer, Inc. can help. Please shoot us an email to yourfriend@friendlyhomebuyer.com, or you can visit our website at www.friendlyhomebuyer.com.

When you're ready, the authors of this book came together to create just for you a 15-point checklist (with pictures) to help maximize your potential and profit in selling your house on your own. You can download a complimentary copy of, **"15 Must-Do Steps to Successfully Selling Your House On Your Own"**, at NoAgentNeeded.com

TO LANDLORD OR NOT?

The Five L's of Real Estate

By
Paul Thompson

Little Rock

I came from a lower, middle-class background. Overall, I had a very pleasant, happy childhood; I was very much loved and cared for. We weren't so poor that I never had anything to eat, clothes to wear, or a place to live. There was just this environment of scarcity; we were not financially prosperous. My parents knew education was my opportunity to do better, so I was encouraged from the very beginning to get a college degree; but it would be up to me to pay for it. So I dutifully followed the conventional wisdom and worked my way through school; I was the first person in my family to graduate with an accredited degree. I earned an engineering degree and landed a respectable job in Little Rock, Arkansas.

With my new income, I jumped a rung in the socioeconomic ladder. I had successfully broken through the lower-income barrier; however, I went through a bit of a depressed phase, which I realized later is common after achieving a long-term goal. I was faced with the reality of having to work for the next forty years. I considered investing in real estate, but I kind of got distracted by the typical American, white-collar lifestyle of working my job, spending my decent salary, buying a house, paying my mortgage, and climbing the corporate ladder.

Periodically, on long weekends or during family vacations, I would think, "Am I doing enough to provide for my future?" I often had a desire to strike out as an entrepreneur, but was afraid of failure and suffered from a lack of knowledge on how to do so. Then I would return to work and again become accustomed to the perceived security of a traditional job. I followed the conventional investing wisdom of saving a little, contributing to the appropriate Qualified Retirement Plan, and investing in the stock market. My goal became: work, save a little, and retire in my 60s.

However, after many years of following this plan, I had to consider how real estate fit into the picture. We upgraded our houses and had to decide what to do with our current house. It's actually not that rare for a family to find themselves with an extra house. Thoughts begin forming: "Should we fix it up and sell it? Should we rent it? What is it really like being a landlord?" And then you think, "How much is all of this is going to cost?"

I had to figure out the same thing. In my case I decided to sell. At the time, I wasn't ready to be a landlord. Your situation might be the same or it might be different. Now I feel much better suited to provide answers when presented with these questions—and after reading this you will too. I've become a full-time real estate investor, and I've helped several people answer this very question for themselves: Should I become a landlord or not?

My First Time Landlording

I've come to realize the decision will NOT primarily come down to money. It will come down to time and energy. You see, being a landlord for one or two houses can take up about as much time as having ten or twelve rental properties.

I'll tell you about my first experience. On my very first deal, I was determined to get into the game. Let me tell you, I had decided it was time to become an investor, and I was going to own a rental property. The deal came from another investor in town. After I viewed the property, I ran my numbers and thought the house would cash flow. We met to sign the deal, and even though I tried to keep a level head, I was so excited I could barely contain it. I tried my hand at negotiating, and when he made a small concession ($1500), I snapped it up.

And then the real life of dealing with property reared its head. I discovered the property's electrical connection wasn't to code, and I incurred almost $1000 to correct it. Then I found out how difficult it is to deal with some utilities. The local municipality has an arcane process that requires your physical presence to file for a business license and turn the power on. After two physical trips to the courthouse and the Electrical coop, I finally managed to take care of it.

Then the rehab ensued. It took twice as long and cost 25 percent more than anticipated. But finally, it was ready to rent. After placing the For-Rent sign in the yard, the phone rang morning and night. Processing and screening all the applicants was very time consuming. Better too many applicants than none at all, I suppose. In a few weeks, the place was rented, and I thought I could finally breathe a sigh of relief. I was looking forward to counting my rent checks as they came in. But then again, I also made the mistake of assuming all the old components of the house would work.

In the ensuing months, the very patient tenant reported legitimate issues with the old heater and the plumbing. When I had purchased the property, I thought I was smart and bought a home warranty. When the heating unit failed, the warranty company gave me the runaround and wouldn't replace the system. Instead, they would horse me around and replace a little component at a time, charging me the deductible per the contract.

I ended up not saving any money by having the warranty. After a few pesky plumbing issues, it became obvious the main sewer line had collapsed, and I had to spend another $3,000 to put in a new cast iron sewer line. Ouch! There's no sizzle in that. It's funny how you plan on putting away little repair reserves with each rent check per month, but then you realize that it takes three to four years of repair reserve allocations to cover $3,000. Double Ouch! This is the opposite of cash flow.

And if that wasn't enough, I hadn't yet learned how to train tenants. The tenant was driving to my home to turn in his rent check. Big bad no-no! Tenants shouldn't know where you live. At that point in my life, however, I was willing to do anything to get that monthly rent payment.

This whole scenario is littered with examples proving I didn't know what I was doing yet. Some of it was bad luck, but I didn't do much to make it any better. The first mistake was that I didn't budget correctly for the rehab, nor did I allocate enough for the ongoing repair numbers. The house was old, and a home warranty isn't a silver bullet for the kind of issues I would most likely have. It never occurred to me the property might not be up to code, nor was I aware of how hard it is to deal with some utilities.

I also realized that when you have tenants who have young children and they don't have running water, you don't have time to shop around for plumbers. The tenant didn't have a working sewer line, and I was pressed for time—especially as I was working a day job and had a family to take care of myself. Beyond that, again, I also failed to train the tenants properly on how, and where, to pay rent. After a few times of meeting the tenant to pick up their payment, the allure of it started to wear off, and the inconvenience of having to deposit the check myself was annoying.

Little mistakes added up, and I compounded them by reacting to the stress and time constraints. Thankfully, none of these issues were showstoppers. It could have been so much worse! This real life example demonstrates why time and energy end up being the driving factors, instead of money.

Recap

Problem 1: I was a buyer not a shopper

Solution:

- Become a bargain shopper and be willing to walk.
- Look for properties that meet your criteria

Problem 2: I was a greenhorn rehabber.

Solution:

- Adjust costs and timelines (assume the worst, not the best).

- If it's not a safe deal, in the worst case scenario, be willing to walk

Problem 3: Naive Landlord

Solution:

- Develop systems to manage and train your tenants to perform per your rules.

Problem 4: Maintenance Issues (What's a Schrader valve?)

Solution:

- Build a team of professionals you trust. Everything can be solved with a phone call.

- Don't do the work yourself. Focus on your job, and it's not being a handyperson.

Problem 5: What have I gotten myself into? (I just wanna go home!)

Solution:

- Relax. Almost everything can be fixed. You can do this if you have enough time and energy.

- You don't have to be a landlord if you don't want to be.

The good news about property is once you get the hang of it—and if you hold the property long enough—you will enjoy the cash flow. I still hold my first property and intend to do so for a very long time. I took each problem as an opportunity to create a solution so that I could either avoid it in the first place or know what to do when it happens again. I learned more through my first investment than I ever could from reading books. This is the real world of real estate investing.

The Five L's of Real Estate

If you are planning on keeping your property and becoming a landlord, you'll need to become a professional. Where I see people going wrong is that they dabble in it. They have just a few houses, do all the work themselves, get worn down over time, and in the end, they swear off owning property. If you feel like that's the situation you'll end up landing in, then sell now. The sooner, the better. Save yourself the time and energy! You can't get the time back, and the lost energy translates to lost opportunity. But if you think you can make a go of it, then learn from my experiences and that of countless others.

From my experiences, I developed my Five L's philosophy:

1. Location
   - Choose the right location

2. Leads
   - Control the lead

3. Leverage
   - Using other people's time and money

4. Landlording
   - Manage the performing asset (directly or indirectly)

5. Liability
   - Minimize liability with insurance and the appropriate legal entities

Location

Most of us realize how important location is in real estate. It gets a lot of attention and rightly so. The one thing I got right with this property is that it's in a solid working class neighborhood. The one aspect of real estate you cannot change is the location. In this case, the prevailing market dynamics indicate this will continue to be a good area. I will be able to ride out the early bumps and enjoy cash flow, in large part, because I'm in a good location.

Leads

This is the aspect where I first went wrong. Having a lot of leads gives you choices. I was too focused on making this deal work. The single greatest lesson I learned from my example is to not fall in love with a property. When it's a house you inherited or a house you used to live in, it's hard to not be emotionally attached to it. If you want to own investment property, don't limit yourself to this one extra house you have; it may not be the right deal for you.

Leverage

Using other people's time and money is common in business. Many people often think of leverage purely as using someone else's money; but it's not just that. You can leverage someone else's time or energy by having them do work. I like to be a capitalist and use other people's human capital—to hire them to do work for me—which is a form of leverage.

In real estate, you can buy an asset using leverage in a way that you can't with most other asset classes. While leveraging other people's money can be one of the greatest aspects of real estate, it can also be the most dangerous, and it's where most investors fail. It's so easy to forget that leverage cuts both ways—this was a big part of the 2008 housing collapse. Where most people tend to run into trouble is in over-leveraging the property; they get in over their heads and can't afford to make the mortgage payments.

In my case, leverage is working for me, and the tenant is paying down my debt with their rental payments—so I'm getting a decent return on the money I put into the rehab. Although it's not been as sweet as I'd hoped it would be, this first property is still a winner, and I've learned innumerable lessons along the way. The takeaway is that I'll just hold this property, and I'll continue to enjoy all the benefits of real estate—even though the cash flow, considering what I first bought it for, isn't quite as much as I'd hoped for.

Landlording

Landlording is just is another way of saying Management—it happens to start with L, which makes for a nice alliteration. You have a couple of choices here. You can self-manage or you can hire a property manager. It can become a philosophic debate whether you handle in-house, outsource to a professional management company, or do a hybrid. Any of these choices work, provided whoever is performing this activity does it well.

I invest locally, in my backyard, so I've chosen to self-manage. I wanted to experience and learn the thrills of management. It can be a demanding and thankless job, but I believe this management process is what controls the actual performing asset. Real estate, in and of itself, doesn't generate income. The people using the real estate are the actual performing asset. Selecting and training tenants (the people using the asset) is what creates the income.

Whether you manage the tenants yourself or manage the property management company, you must choose wisely. This is not a responsibility you can abdicate because, either way, if you aren't careful, tenants will manage you. I've learned a lot on this subject and have become a much more effective manager. When done correctly, property management is not that hard, but you must learn how to do it well.

To begin with, you must screen appropriately. I have only three requirements of a tenant: (1) pay on time every time, (2) take care of the property, and (3) stay forever. I don't think that's too much to ask, do you?

In all seriousness, I've learned the first rule is that I don't collect rent. Tenant's pay or they don't stay. One great tip I learned is to just give tenants deposit slips for my checking account and have them go to the bank and deposit the check themselves. I no longer accept hand- delivered cash, money orders, or checks. I give tenants two payment options: (1) they can pay automatically and receive a discount, or (2) they can pay their rent manually at the nearest bank branch. Either way, the responsibility is in their hands and removes me from the equation.

Management 101! Eliminate, automate, delegate! *Eliminate* me from the equation, *automate* the payment for a discount, or *delegate* responsibility to the tenant to make the payment. And if no payment is made by the fifth of the month, the eviction process automatically starts. The policy is nonnegotiable, and it is completely automated. My tenant from my first landlording property now religiously pays on time using automatic draft. I haven't had any further issues from them.

I've also significantly reduced my management overhead by defining what a tenant should contact me about. I give each tenant an emergency contact list. They have the contact information for my handyperson, plumber, HVAC contractor, and locksmith. I've trained both the tenants and the contractors on what the rules of engagement are, as well as when and how I need to be notified—most of which is by email.

If you take away anything from this chapter on whether you should be a landlord or not, remember that property management is what will determine your success. Be honest with yourself! If you won't put in the time to effectively manage the tenants or your property manager, then owning real estate is not for you.

Liability

The big fear with liability is getting pulled into a frivolous lawsuit. This is one of the subjects that often receives too much attention. While asset protection is a viable concern—because we have become such a litigious society—lawsuits remain one the lowest risks for the average investor. A complex asset-protection scheme should be reserved until an investor develops a significant amount of assets. Instead, investors should carry good liability insurance as the first line of defense.

Make sure not to overlook the low cost of umbrella policies because they offer a great protection for very low premiums. Now that LLC's (limited liability companies) have been adopted in all fifty states, it has become very easy to establish a liability shield for a moderately low start-up cost. An investor should hold their assets in the appropriate entity for their situation and enjoy the protection of personal assets from business activities. Seek appropriate counsel on all legal and tax matters for specific recommendations.

If you've decided NOT to be a landlord and cash out instead, my company buys houses in Central Arkansas. To receive a fair and reasonable offer from us in as little as 24 hours, please contact me at paul@wincorehomes.com, or visit us at www.wincorehomes.com.

THE HOME RUN DEAL THAT WASN'T

By
Todd Toback

San Diego

I started buying houses back in 2000. I remember driving up to California with $300 in my pocket, and I was really excited about getting started on this new direction. While I did have an amazing job (I was actually working for Pfizer, selling Viagra, during the heyday when it first launched), I realized that I didn't want to work in corporate America anymore. It was a lot of fun during that time, but after spending two years with Pfizer, I decided that it really wasn't for me—and I had this itch to get into real estate.

Really, the catapulting factor was when I asked my boss for a promotion and a raise. He was very, very nice; but he spoke to me like a father does to a child and said, "Hey, you know, you don't understand how the corporate world works. You can't just ask for, you know, a big raise and get it. It takes time and politics, and it's a systematic process, and you gotta pay your dues." He basically said, "No," and I was really embarrassed after our meeting. I got in my Chevy Impala, a little dejected, and started making my way home.

I was on the 101 freeway, right in the Ventura, California, Oxnard area, and I saw a Barnes & Noble on the right. I remember I was about three lanes over from the exit and something just said, "Hey, you've gotta pull over and go in that bookstore." I immediately pulled over three lanes—everyone honking their horns and giving me the finger— and I made it off the freeway and into the shopping center. I bought a book on real estate and I read the whole thing, cover to cover, in one night. In that book, I read that I should send out mail pieces to the property owners in my area, specifically, to those who might live elsewhere (out-of-state owners). I sent out a bunch of letters, and forty-five days later I bought my first piece of real estate in a small beach town in Carpinteria, California. I was scared to death; I had no idea how to make it work.

The truth was that I didn't have any money when I first started. I really didn't know what I was doing, so I had to get a money partner who would help me buy the house, turn it around, and make a profit;

sixteen years later, we've done close to 1000 deals. During that time, I married my high school sweetheart, and we now homeschool our four children.

I love helping sellers solve real estate challenges and move on to the next phase of their life. I've purchased all kinds of houses, big and small, and I've had some pretty nasty tenant situations. We don't really focus on buying houses; instead, we focus on solving problems, creating solutions, and really helping people relieve their stress and all the negative emotions associated with selling their houses—a lot of stress/anxiety comes with the process.

Landfill, El Cajon

There's one particular deal that comes to mind, one of the craziest and gnarliest deals, in El Cajon, California. An agent named Victoria called me up said, "Hey Todd, I've got this great piece of real estate that's worth $415K, but you can buy it for $181K." She then informed me, "The only thing is the property borders a landfill, and so, for whatever reason, it can't get financing."

I said, "Okay. No big deal. Let me take a look at it."

I took a look, and it seemed like it'd be sound; I thought it'd be a home run deal, spreading between $181K and $450K. It felt like I couldn't lose. After we bought the property, we were pretty sure we'd immediately make a killing; we were really, really excited, "This is gonna be amazing!" The house was already rented to some tenants and, after owning it for a short time, we gave them notice to move; but they were really attached to the property. They wanted to buy it. We did, in fact, offer to sell it to them; however, as Victoria had told me, they couldn't get a bank loan or any financing because of the landfill.

Angry at the situation, the tenants totally stopped paying rent. They started making up all these repairs, telling crazy stories about us. When we went to make repairs, they would end up calling the police. So, they were requesting repairs, and then not allowing us inside when we went to the property. All of a sudden, they'd claim there was toxic mold; but again, they wouldn't let us in. Then they started sending letters that the property was toxic which was getting them sick. Victoria, the agent, was correct in that the landfill was a non-issue, but the tenants used the law to their advantage and continued living on the property, all the while claiming it was toxic. We went to court, and they kept finding delays on delays on delays before the judge could even hear the case. The tenants kept maneuvering their way through the legal system without any kind of merit. They lived on the property for close to a year, rent-free.

Finally, when the judge actually heard the case, he determined the property was safe to live in and that nothing was wrong with it; in fact, it was a great property. The judge ordered the tenants to pay all back rent, as well as our legal fees. Unfortunately, if you know anything about the legal system, if you win in court and a judge says you win, it's just a piece of paper. We never saw any of that twelve months' rent. We never saw any of the $62K that we paid in legal fees. At that, the tenants totally thrashed the place, costing us a year of stress, aggravation, and a lot of money. All in all, we lost over $100K.

Lessons Learned

Knowing the situation now, and the tenants, I should've been more conservative in buying the house. It looked like a great deal, but there were many factors, and there was a reason why the owner was willing to sell. I should've consulted an attorney before trying to evict—it's never black and white. The law does, in fact, favor tenants, especially in California, so you really need to be careful when you're evicting—*don't try to do it yourself.*

The tenants proceeded to use some of the defects of the house to delay the process, withhold rent, and distort the facts. If you have bad tenants, be prepared for a massive battle. It's not as easy as filing paperwork. You can't just knock on the door and kick them out; it costs time, money, energy, hassle, and again, the law is on their side. If you're a landlord (you have a house and you have tenants), you can't just assume that by serving them a piece of paper, they'll move out; it's a lot more complicated than that. If you do it the wrong way, your tenants can stay for a really, really, really, really long time; this might end up costing you a lot of money, well beyond the lost rent.

The great thing about this deal was the original seller who sold us the property; they were really excited they were able to do this deal. They actually moved up north, leaving us their tenants—true gifts—and they lived happily ever after; I was happy that we could help them. The property, itself, required a major, major fix up after the tenants moved out. We then sold it for a profit, but not for nearly as much as we thought we would; however, we made it out and the seller was happy, so that was neat.

Part of my recipe for success is perseverance. When you've got a deal, you need to see it all the way through. When you agree to a deal with a seller, you need to ensure that you can help them, close the deal, provide their money, and do what you said you would do.

As a professional, you need a good lawyer. If you're going to get into this business, you also need the willingness to take on the bad guy; there are some unscrupulous characters out there, and that's just part of a cost of doing business. *Do not get jaded.* Remember, *we're in this business to help people.*

From this Carpinteria property, I learned that a home run is never a home run until the property is sold. Many sellers think, "We're gonna make a killing because we're gonna buy a property $100,000 below market!" But that's not even close to what you make. Actually, you won't even make a fraction of that. Often you'll see yourself losing on a deal, especially after your time is factored. As a matter of fact, one of the reasons why we made money on that house was because the market went up during that whole process. If it hadn't, we wouldn't have.

I've also learned to communicate with sellers on the benefits of doing business with us, while also sharing some of my challenges. Often, people have tenants in the property and they think it's no big deal; they have repairs and they don't think that it will cost that much; or they think that the selling time is inconsequential. Please note: all of those factors are much more important than some might think.

Once you calculate the legal cost, tenants, repairs, fees, insurance, lawyers, real estate commissions, and holding costs, you won't net nearly as much as you think with an agent versus just selling to an investor—like myself. Many sellers think investors make a ton of money when we buy a property, and we do, but not nearly as much as they think. Sometimes investors win and then, sometimes we don't. We lose money all the time, and that's just part of business. The great thing is that when you're a professional and you do the right thing and your sellers are happy, they will then give you testimonials—you always win.

Instead of immediately going to a legal battle, we did try to gracefully negotiate with the tenants a win-win solution; that works sometimes, but not all the time. We got a great lawyer, but we also remained calm and understood that legal fees are sometimes the cost of doing this business. If you have a partner involved (like we did on this deal), avoid arguing and infighting; we stuck together, got the deal closed, and that's really important. If you have tenants who are already in the property (bad tenants at that), it's not about collecting the back rent; you probably won't see a dime of that. Getting the property vacant, empty, and sold should be your highest priority, because that's when you'll actually make the money.

Once your property is vacant, you'll want to rehab it fast. You should stage it, and when you do, you should let professionals do that;

in doing so, you should find the best agent to list if you are not doing it alone. For this particular home, we spent about $50K to get it up and running. The one thing about this property is that we had to make it look pristine, so a great buyer could live there.

Problem:

Tenants were determined to live rent free and extort money from the new owners (us).

Our solution:

1. We tried to gracefully negotiate the tenants a win-win solution.
2. We found appropriate legal counsel.
3. We remained calm and understood that legal fees are sometimes a cost of doing business.
4. We stuck together with our partner.
5. We understood that getting a property vacant was not about the money owed to us.
   - Getting it ready for sale was the highest priority.
6. Once vacant, we rehabbed it fast, staged it, and found the best agent to list it.
   - We spent about $50K to get this property back in shape.
7. We offered a great product to an end buyer and we made a profit.

Our original seller was ecstatic once he heard about the ordeal we'd had to go through. He was sorry to hear about our conflict, but he said, "I'm so glad I'm not in your shoes." Our job was to take that away from him—the stress, the time, and the energy—and give him the opportunity to be happy with his family up north, which he really appreciated.

The website for our house-buying business is www.getitdone housebuyers.com. If you're looking to sell your house in greater San Diego county, that's the website to go to.

When you're ready, the authors of this book came together to create just for you a 15-point checklist (with pictures) to help maximize your potential and profit in selling your house on your own. You can download a complimentary copy of, **"15 Must-Do Steps to Successfully Selling Your House On Your Own"**, at NoAgentNeeded.com

INSTANT UNWANTED LANDLORD, HELP!

By
Drew Hitt

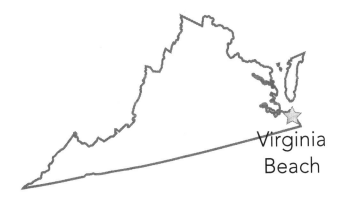

Virginia Beach

I started my business twelve years ago. It took a good two years to feel like I had "learned enough" to take action, so I like to say I officially started it ten years ago. I've been married to my wife, Jessica, for eleven years. Together, we have the world's best nine-year-old daughter, Taylor, and a Labradoodle named Sampson who officially loves the girls more than he loves me. I love my family, and I love building the business, serving both my employees and my customers.

Most importantly, I love the time I get to spend with my daughter. Whether it's "Playground Hopping" as we call it (involving visits to several local playgrounds in the area and playing on each of them together), or doing our "Daddy-Daughter" days, it's the best time of the week, being with her while she still can tolerate her "embarrassing dad." I'm still trying to learn how to dance to the rhythm of music—it's harder than you think!

The Inheritance

My company used to send a thousand postcards a month or so to reach anyone interested in selling and get them to pick up the phone and call us. We now send tens of thousands of postcards a month. I had a particular call where a seller recently inherited a house from her father, and it came with tenants of roughly twenty years. The seller was looking to sell the property so she wouldn't have to deal with it. As with most sellers who work with us, she owned the house free and clear, but was not prepared to deal with the situation. She called me up, I took the call personally, and we set an appointment for a visit to the property so I could see its condition.

Later that day, we met up to walk the place and come up with a solution to her situation. As we spoke, I realized that another investor in my market had made the seller an all-cash offer on the house, so I had to be competitive or creative. Since I didn't want to discuss a personal matter like selling the house right there in front of the tenants, we decided to take the appointment back to her house a couple of miles down the street.

Once we arrived there, we started talking. Honestly, we spoke less about the house and more about the results she wanted to see, what she wanted, and just about life in general. It all came down to the fact that it wasn't necessarily about the cash; she just wanted to know that things would be taken care of and that the tenant would be handled properly. She confided in me that she liked me more than the other investor, and that she thought I handled everything professionally; she appreciated that I was educating her on the process.

I saw her property as a prime rental in a great location, so I wanted to keep it for as long as possible. Because my vision was aligned with her needs, I made an almost full-price offer on her house. I proposed she take the money in installments because an all-cash offer wasn't important to her; she just wanted to feel like she got as much as possible out of the house.

The challenge of this deal was breaking the news to the tenants of over twenty years. Fair market rent on the place was probably $1,200 a month and the tenants were paying $520; that was barely enough to cover taxes and insurance on the property, let alone maintenance and profit. It's not easy to have a conversation with a tenant, as they've turned a rental into a home, and they've watched their children grow up in their home.

I had to delicately approach the situation and have a frank conversation with them on what could they afford, while giving them enough time to move on, if necessary. Not only had they been in the house for twenty years, it didn't look like they'd gotten rid of anything within that time frame. Needless to say, the house was packed—not quite hoarder status, but a ton of stuff.

Honestly, some of the mistakes in this deal really just came down to the length of time the tenants would need to pack up and move on, which was sixty days. Also, it was hard explaining to the seller how the deal would work in terms she could easily understand; in this case, she would be the bank. With her being the bank, she wanted a ton of money to be put down. While it's not as much money now, back then, when I was just getting started, $45K was a *huge* amount to me.

Some of the biggest mistakes I see people making in this business are rooted in forgetting that this is a people business, where it's all about the seller, and it almost never has anything to do with us, the buyer. We should always treat everyone like they are our own mother, father, or grandparents; treat them with respect and honesty; and help them at every opportunity. In this business, the process of selling a house holds people back from better things and moving forward in their lives; until this burden or obstacle is removed, they are stuck in that situation.

There were two aspects to this deal that made it successful:

1. The necessary actions taken in solving the seller's problems
2. The tenants

For the seller, it wasn't about getting all her cash now; it was about feeling like she got a great price so her money could last as long as possible. This house was the only true wealth that her father left her, and taking the low cash offer made by the other investor didn't sit well with her. She wanted to feel like she got a deal, that I got a deal, and everyone could win in this situation. So, because I knew it was about price with her, I took the following actions:

A. I offered her about 10 percent below market value if she would take the money in monthly payments
B. I presented her with a few scenarios, so she could pick whichever approach she felt worked best for her situation.

Since she was still working full time, she felt the highest price with the most money down was her best option. My offer was $190K, with $45K down, and a favorable payment schedule for the rest of the money. We both agreed the house would probably be worth $210K—if it was completely fixed up, and if it didn't need a ton of work. The inside of the house was entirely 1960s. However, what happened next, I *never* would have expected. I was perfectly happy with this offer; but that's when the seller surprised me.

She said, "Drew, I want you to get a good deal here, too."

I responded, "I'm comfortable with this offer. If I wasn't, I certainly wouldn't have made it."

"I like you," she said, "and I want you to get a great deal. So I'll take $135,000 with the same agreement."

Now I was shocked. I reminded her I was comfortable with my original offer; but she insisted—and after all, the customer is always right! We agreed, and she signed the agreement.

Then it came to the tenants. When I spoke with them, it was clear that they were very understanding as they knew the old owner had passed away. They were very much aware that they were getting a deal on rent. Their biggest concern was having enough time to find a proper place (sixty days) because the husband was bedridden in the living room. As I'd previously dealt with somewhat similar situations, I knew the most important thing was listening to their needs, understanding what they wanted, and helping make the transition easy. I was also aware that I needed to know what their budget might be, too, in order to assist them in finding a new place to live.

I ended up hiring some friends of mine to help them move all their things. I paid for a U-Haul truck for them to use and helped them find a new place. In the end, it took them a little over a month to find a place, as well as move everything. I didn't ask them to clean at all, just to take what they wanted and leave the rest for us to handle. As they didn't have a security deposit, I wasn't worried about the condition of the house when they left.

My company strives to make the transaction as easy as possible for all parties; the easier the better, that's why we're such a great alternative to real estate agents—the ease of the transaction. In this case, we worked with both the tenants of twenty years and the seller, and as a result, the seller ended up with a big chunk of money, and she felt secure. I ended up with a great rental property, after I fixed it up, one that would serve me well for years to come.

Lessons Learned

- In this business, it's not about what's in it for me.
  - It's about the best solution for the seller's situation.
    - Even when I deliver what I believe is the right solution, sellers still surprise me.

- It's not about price.
  - It has more to do with how you treat that client.
    - At the end of the day, the seller didn't like the other investor's approach; on the other hand, the seller and I felt like old friends.

- Our service solves a huge problem out there for property owners.
  - Unforeseen problems fall right in their laps.
    - It takes someone like us to come in, help by walking them through the process, and then offer multiple solutions to whatever their issues are.

We spent close to $25K fixing the house up. We replaced the appliances, re-did the flooring, and renovated both bathrooms completely. We also painted the interior of the house and replaced all the windows. The property itself needed a ton of landscaping; the house sat on a large lot, and there were overgrown trees and vegetation that needed to be removed in order to make the yard usable. We also finished the garage-conversion, so it was properly conditioned to be used as livable space. My father-in-law did all of this for us as he had a small crew of guys who would work along with him on our projects. Beyond that, we needed to a hire a plumber to fix a lot of the plumbing problems under the house.

We went overboard with the master bathroom. We installed travertine-looking tiles halfway up the walls and on the shower floor. In the bathroom, we added a new bath and replaced the flooring and toilets—not everyone loves a pink-and-blue bathroom! The house was also in need of a HVAC unit, so we found a contractor to replace it. We ended up overpaying quite a bit on that, so we now have a contractor that's been with us for seven years whom I wouldn't trade for the world—good contractors are golden!

Once the work was finished, we put the house up for rent at almost double what it was originally rented for. Through a combination of yellow signs around the neighborhood and posting the property every week on craigslist.com, we ended up finding a great couple who stayed a few years. We just recently turned the property over again, after our third set of tenants. We did not fare as well on that round: we needed to completely replace damaged doors, as well as the one-year-old carpets which were ruined, and the place was flea and roach infested. So not all tenants are the same. We ended up spending another $4,000 fixing and repainting the place to get it rentable again; however, it's currently up for rent for a little over $1,400.

Our original problem was an inherited property with inherited tenants paying a super-discounted rent. Our solution was to create a plan for the seller that would also work with the tenants, so both could feel comfortable when all the dust settled. When I tell this story, I like pointing out that another investor involved in the picture just didn't have the answer to this dilemma. Just as the seller wanted, I found us a plan where everyone won. And just as my company continues to strive for, we did our best to make the transaction easy.

If you want to know what I can do for you to maximize your profit through creative solutions on your Viriginia property, please contact me at Drew@HamptonRoadsCashHomeBuyer.com or online at www.HamptonRoadsCashHomeBuyer.com.

FATAL FOURPLEX

By
Omar Merced

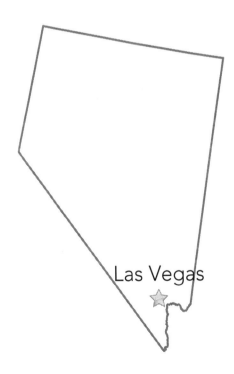

I joined the Army after my seventeenth birthday. I came in with the delayed-entry program; I did basic training during the summer, returned to finish high school, and then finished with advanced individual training (AIT) after graduation. I was trained as a combat medic. After AIT, I went back to Puerto Rico to attend a University—I didn't last even a semester; it wasn't the right time, and I wasn't prepared, at all. I've always been able to grasp things rather quickly, but I am also a procrastinator, which is something I have only just begun managing effectively.

After two years in Puerto Rico trying to figure things out, I went active duty. My next job in the military would be working on the armament and electrical systems of the AH-64A Apache aka Armament Dawg. I was stationed in Fort Campbell, Kentucky for my first assignment. I attended Air Assault School—that's the one where you rappel out of a helicopter, among other things. I was deployed to Kuwait. It was my first time out of the country, and it really opened my eyes. Afterward, I had a series of assignments and eventually got accepted to the rotary wing training program at Fort Rucker, Alabama. While learning to fly, I found my love on the ground in real estate, and over the next fifteen years, I was involved with many different types of real estate dealings. I've seen some very creative ways to make deals work.

Americana Slice

I was newly married at the time. My now ex-wife and I decided to purchase a house. We started looking for the perfect starter home and spent some time trying to find it. In the summer of our search, I saw a For Sale By Owner (FSBO) sign in front of a fourplex. It was a Midwest property. The grass was a little high, but the building was in generally good condition. It wasn't anything particularly exciting or flashy; it just looked like a solid apartment. Overall, I saw a clean building and a generally well-maintained surrounding area. It was painted yellow-beige with white trim. Nothing was exaggerated, it just looked like a slice of Americana—a good place to live.

The FSBO sign caught my attention because I thought (you know...) we wouldn't need to use an agent. I thought that was a good thing. Standing there with our car parked in front of the building, I looked at the units and I realized that we could live in one and rent out the other three at about $500 each (which was the going rate back then). I knew what the mortgage amount would've been, and that there would be a lot of cash flow left. It just made perfect sense—or so I thought. While I saw the opportunity, I didn't take into account the emotional part of buying real estate.

If you have a partner, being on the same page is important. I don't think this can be overstated; it's true in business as much as it is in life. If you don't share a similar vision, everything is harder. This difference of opinion turned what should've been a celebration into a real estate nightmare. Your vision must be shared and talked about. It's important to understand that everyone is raised with different values, life goals, and concepts of making a living. Once you understand this, only then can you create a shared vision for you and your partner. This was the first of the many mistakes I would make on my journey.

I knew nothing about real estate back then. I simply looked at this fourplex and said to myself, "They rent for $500 each, and since there would be three tenants, that means I'll get $1,500 per month." It made "perfect" sense to me, and I thought it would make sense to anyone looking at it; but that was not the case—this was not how the other party was looking at this. In hindsight, there were so many other things I should've taken into account—like turnover cost, vacancy, tenant issues, capital expenditures, property management, etc.—but this one was mine, and I was going to have it, no matter the cost.

For most people who look at real estate, I think we let emotions get the best of us. We negotiate on behalf of the deal. I think that is the most dangerous thing a real estate investor can do.

My then-wife and I started the journey looking for a home to live in and enjoy (as we all are trained and convinced to do from an early age). She was looking for The American Dream. She could not grasp how living in a two-bedroom apartment would prepare us for the future, and she fought me along every single step, refusing to sign anything. Still, I persisted with the purchase and I eventually convinced her to sign on the dotted line. The fourplex was officially ours; however, we never moved into that apartment because doing so would prove too emotional for my partner.

On the bright side, I was lucky to have a property manager in place, and a good one, at that. They helped me take care of the maintenance required; the unit we were supposed to move into was rented out and had very little turnover during the next few years. It netted about $800–$900 per month, and I did hardly anything; as far as I was concerned, the fourplex was a great investment, and I loved owning it. Looking back, I realized I had purchased the property without walking all the units, relying on my own visual inspection to determine whether they were in good shape. So I didn't use a home inspector, which, in hindsight, wasn't actually the best idea—in fact, it was crazy. This was my first property, and I didn't know anything. I was brand new to the actual process and cost involved. One of my wake-up calls happened after one of the tenants moved and I was left holding a $2,500 rehab bill to get the property back to rent-ready condition. *Let the contracting begin . . .*

After a call from another tenant, we had to replace some of the appliances, which were outdated anyway. Once again, the property manager took care of it. They coordinated the delivery and installation. This was really simple for me; and at that, it was all for a rental, so I didn't have any emotional attachment. To me it was just business.

In regard to contractors, most homeowners get a bid, compare some prices, and make sure the material is the desired quality; if it is, then they sign a contract. Most often, a minimal deposit will be needed for material, and then the contractor comes in and does the work. Keep in mind that before you hire anyone, it's important to find your contractor from a referral source, or be certain they're well vetted to lessen your chances of getting burned.

The fourplex already had a property manager, so aside from all the headaches and fights to get the deal closed, the management part was a pretty seamless transition. Most often, property managers' interests don't actually align with the homeowner's; always check whether their maintenance is in-house or out-of-house. Some property management companies have a practice of sending maintenance people for their own benefit, as opposed to that of their clients; this is one of the biggest problems I've seen in property management.

I was lucky, but I should have done my due diligence before hiring a property manager. There are many other situations where the tides can turn against the homeowner. As it turned out, I ended up being a property manager, myself, in the course of my journey through real estate.

Lessons Learned

After the fact, I'm well aware of what I should've known and done because I didn't do it. Now, I know that you should most definitely do your due diligence. You should read through contracts (yes, the long, boring contracts) with property management, and make sure you're not getting into anything that you are not aware of. Make sure they don't have a clause in there giving them the first right of refusal to list the property, which is a pretty common practice among property management companies; if they do, then negotiate that before signing.

These details are usually in the property management agreement, along with the commissions and other expenses related to the sale of your home.

Forecasting expenses is a big part of this. People live in their homes, always reacting to things—just living life, waiting for something to happen, and then responding to it. A lot of people don't give thought to putting money away; but in this business and in life, establishing a little reserve is vital for your "capital expenditures" (in reference to something like your air-conditioning going out, or your roof or siding needing updates or replacement). Do you want the premium price for your property? If so, then you need to address these things; if you don't address them, then the first thing to come out in negotiation is the buyer addressing them and telling you exactly how much their cost is.

The buyer's bids are usually higher than yours because they're not looking at it from the same angle as you. So, it is your responsibility to know these details: how long your roof or siding will last; how old your air-conditioner or water heater is. On that note, water heaters, in particular, are a very common issue after a few years of owning a property.

If you decide to use property management, then you should look at their statements monthly, so that you can regularly ensure they are as accurate as possible; that income will directly affect the sale of the property, if it's a rental property. You'll know how long the lease is, and when you're going over those monthly expenses, you just need to look for anything out of the norm. Within the first couple of months, you should talk to your property manager to be sure you understand every expense on the sheet and exactly how it's related to you and your property, including how that expense directly correlates to your success in leasing. You also need to check your contract when you sell your property. Will your contract with the property manager become null and void, or is that contract part of the property?

When selling real estate, always anticipate your "turnover" cost. Most often, you'll need to put some money into the property in order to sell it. If at all possible, in order to get the best bang for your buck (the best price per square foot), you need to address, at a minimum, all the deferred maintenance you may not have gotten around to. Then, if possible, you should address all cosmetic details; in fact, one of the easiest and most cost-efficient options is painting the entire home. Carpeting isn't too bad dollarwise. One of the more expensive options is replacing

tile in kitchens and bathrooms; at that point, you'll need to evaluate the cost of the renovation versus the amount expected in return.

If you don't put money aside for turnover costs, it can become unexpectedly expensive. The hope is that you have either the money put away to be able to handle these expenses or enough equity in the home to be able to pull out some money to do these repairs. It's best to handle these things intelligently, so you can recoup the money. If you're trying to sell a multi-family unit, then you'll need to multiply that cost by however many units are involved.

Telling your tenants you're selling the property is up to you; but as soon as anyone comes by to take a look, they'll most likely figure it out. Tenants react differently. Ideally, you have a harmonious building where everybody gets along. I definitely believe communication can affect how they respond. If you have one bad tenant who is not picking up after themselves, leaving trash everywhere, you should address that before you put the property on the market—always consider the importance of curb appeal.

All of that in mind, you should get rid of as much as possible. Plan what you'll move with you. What do you really want to take to your next house? In life, we accumulate a lot of things over time; a great idea is throwing some yard or garage sales and posting on all the local sites like craigslist and OfferUp. Do your best to get rid of as much stuff and recoup as much money as you can from it. Make an offset on some of the maintenance cost or some of the landscaping cost, while also ensuring your home is free of clutter.

When it comes to the sale, you need to emotionally detach yourself from the process. It's very hard removing all the pictures of you and your family, cleaning out, and decluttering. In order to sell for the highest price, you'll need to remove emotion from that equation as much as possible. If the buyer says the property looks terrible, but they make you a good offer, you need to decide if the physical capital they're trying to give to you is worth more than the emotional capital you've invested in your home.

You're selling one of your biggest assets. It's where you and usually your family have lived for a few years. You've made some great memories in that home; you've had some good and bad times. You remember the day you bought it, how it was closing the deal. You have all this emotional baggage attached to this house. When you're selling your property you just need to be aware of that aspect and to do your best to remove yourself from it, to understand that you're doing this so that another family or another investor can enjoy the property, while you move on to a different chapter in your life. The market is the market and it couldn't care less about the either the buyer or seller's feelings. It is what it is, and it always is.

Why am I sharing all of this with you? Because my actions and lack thereof with regard to my one-sided desire for maximizing my investment ultimately lead to my property going into foreclosure. My then-wife and I went through a horrible divorce, and what started wrong ended wrong. The property manager eventually refused to manage the fourplex, and the bank took the property back and sold it. It didn't matter because I knew what real estate could do; I was hooked and still am.

Problem:

Not having your partner share your vision will hamper your results

Solutions:

A. Share your "why" with your partner.

B. Understand your partner's "why."

C. Discuss your obstacles and objections, and try to understand the different points of view.

D. Come up with solutions together.

From this fourplex, I learned the importance of keeping open and consistent communication with my partner. We should have been on the same page from the beginning, and because we weren't, it made everything feel like pushing a car uphill. Honestly, there was nothing wrong with the property; there was something wrong with me. I didn't take into account the emotional cost that goes into buying, maintaining, and selling a property.

This was my first lesson in owning real estate, and it taught me many things. It showed me that if you want something, don't give up. It showed me what a good property manager looks like, what to look for in monthly statements, what things cost, how to forecast expenses, and the pride of ownership. It showed me that a well-run property can get you to financial freedom. Most importantly, it showed me how much emotion can influence a transaction; if you want to do this right, then you need to keep those emotions in check.

If you want my company, Real Estate Wishes, to help you explore all of your options around selling or keeping your Las Vegas property, please contact me at (702) 706-7160, Omar@RealEstateWishes.com, or visit our website at www. RealEstateWishes.com

When you're ready, the authors of this book came together to create just for you a 15-point checklist (with pictures) to help maximize your potential and profit in selling your house on your own. You can download a complimentary copy of, **"15 Must-Do Steps to Successfully Selling Your House On Your Own"**, at NoAgentNeeded.com

SUBJECT TO OPTIONS

A Dodd-Frank Nightmare

By
Stuart Gethner, RPh

Phoenix

I was born in Chicago to a family of health-care professionals and real estate entrepreneurs. I received both my undergraduate and graduate degrees in political science and pharmacology. Married. Three great kids. Four dogs. Couple of cats and some horses. I'm a full-time real estate investor.

I own a real estate investment firm in Phoenix, Arizona called Phelps Capital and Consulting Inc., as well as a property management company called Dobson Real Property Management, LLC. We do a fair amount of marketing, and many of our leads come through the telephone. We received a call one day from a gal named Judy, who explained that her mom, Karen, was ill and had been hospitalized; Karen was elderly, in her late sixties, early seventies. And while Karen was in the hospital, her home had gone uncared for. Now that she was discharged, Judy and the rest of her family realized the house was actually too much for Karen to take care of alone—the landscaping was out of hand, and overall, the house itself was too big.

Their family had been raised there, and not only was it time for Karen to move on, she already had moved on; she moved out when she got back to the house and realized it was too big. Now she was renting a two-bedroom apartment elsewhere, and her limited income was being diverted to the new apartment for the security deposit and other expenses—so she was falling behind on expenses for her house, which was entering foreclosure.

Judy was a little bit in panic mode. She didn't want her mom to have a foreclosure on her record, nor did she want the house to get much more dilapidated. The family was also concerned about squatters and what have you. They wondered whether we would come out and take a look, and possibly be interested in the house. So it was a good situation for us because we had a seller who could use our help, and the house (other than being dated) was in pretty good shape—up to that point, their mom had surely been taking care of it.

The house had plenty of deferred maintenance, but it was not trashed. Other than the landscaping and a sort of renaissance-like-scent when you walked in—it smelled and looked like the proverbial "grandma's house," in which "grandma" was a cigarette smoker to boot—along with the counter tops and such needing some work, it wasn't bad; we recognized the situation: All they really wanted was to get mom out of foreclosure.

There's a strategy we use in real estate investing called "Subject-To." This is a short paraphrase for the expression "subject to the existing financing," which is a legal term. Simply put, it means I'll take over your payments, and you can leave the house. So, the deed goes to me. The loan stays in your name, until sold or refinanced, while I care for the property and make your payments.

In a traditional real estate transaction, there's a marriage of the loan and the deed. The deed gets recorded, and that deed is what gives someone title to the property. So, in a Subject-To transaction they actually get divorced. The deed transfers to someone else's name, yet the loan stays in that borrower's name. So why would anybody do that? Why would anybody give the deed of their house to someone else, yet leave the note and the loan in their own name? The answer to that—they have to move fast.

So in similar situations, I've done this before. Some folks get a job transfer and they have to move right away; however, if the house has a lot of value to it, if there's a lot of equity in it, then it doesn't make sense for the seller to do a Subject-To—they should just stick a signpost in the ground and sell it. But in a situation where what's owed is close to the value, and the house needs some work, these scenarios might be a motivation for someone to just want to walk away. And that's what we had here.

We found out the amount of the loan balance. Would we be able to take it over for the loan balance? There was actually a few dollars of equity in it, and we thought it was possibly a great opportunity for us to fix it up and then, either keep it as a rental or flip it. And when we fully evaluated it, we decided we would keep it as a rental and take it over (subject to the existing financing). So, we got all the paperwork in order, Judy introduced us to Karen, and we did the transaction. I presented a Subject-To purchase contract, in which the purchase price was the current loan balance. The house would make a *perfect* rental property in our portfolio: three-bedroom, two-bath, corner lot, and there were schools within walking distance, as well as shopping, churches, and the freeway in close proximity.

The monthly PITI (principal, interest, taxes, insurance) payment was just under seven hundred dollars. We believed we could rent the property for twelve hundred dollars a month! We knew we needed about five thousand dollars for paint, newer fixtures, and cleanup costs to get the house rent-ready. We would have all our out-of-pocket expenses back within the first year!

Karen signed the contract, and we opened escrow! She and Judy were so relieved, and I was ecstatic to get a *great* rental property in my portfolio with little to no money down! Karen signed the paperwork, and then we went to the title company and opened escrow—*everything* you do goes through a title company because they are the impartial referee ensuring everybody's protected and no one's taken advantage of in the escrow instructions. After escrow was opened, we asked for prepossession to get the property rent-ready. It was at that point the title company informed us that Karen bought this property with a FHA (Federal Housing Administration) loan. That was no big deal to us as we've taken over conventional, FHA, and VA (Veterans Affairs) loans in the past; regardless of the type of loan, we can purchase a property Subject-To.

The title company educated us that since the fiasco in 2008, FHA changed some rules. And one of the rules they changed now made it illegal to take over an FHA loan or *any* government loan Subject-

To. And we just didn't know that. Having done many Subject-To transactions with this title company before, I thought they were joking.

From the Dodd-Frank Act was born the Consumer Financial Protection Bureau (CFPB). They were given unyielding power to protect consumers from the financial sector. The title company mentioned the CFPB has only two offices in the United States—and one of them is in Phoenix! The title company went on to further educate me on issues specific to this transaction. If I were to close this transaction myself and record the deed, it would then be difficult to get title insurance, after the fact. So, closing the transaction outside of a title company could be done, but was not a viable solution.

I didn't have the heart to call Judy or Karen on the phone and inform them that their transaction was no longer in my sweet spot. We promised Karen that (a) we would get her out of foreclosure, (b) spend a few thousand bucks to back up the late payments, (c) spend the money to make sure the landscaping was done, and (d) take it over and use it as a quality rental. But there wasn't enough money in it to just stick a signpost in the ground and sell it for Karen because it didn't have enough equity. And so, we put ourselves in this bind by just not knowing that the rules had changed.

With that said, we felt bad backing out. And we could have backed out; but it would have been the wrong thing to do because Karen already moved on with her life. Her property was an albatross around her neck and it was really weighing her down; working with us and having us sign the paperwork was a huge sigh of relief for her. So, I very much felt that going back to her and saying "we can't do this anymore because we didn't know you had a FHA loan and we didn't know the laws had changed" just wasn't who I wanted to be.

So, we tried to think of a way that we could (a) still control the property, (b) get it off her hands, (c) be responsible for it, (d) take that liability and stress off her shoulders—and (e) still come out ahead in the long run. I slept on it for a night or so and I came up with an idea: *buy the house from her on a Lease-Option.*

Lease-Option Solution

The mistake I made was not educating myself or keeping myself updated on relevant industry information. I previously believed that the Dodd-Frank Act was specific to owner-occupied residential real estate. Though I was purchasing residential real estate, I was doing it as a business. Hence, it is commercial real estate to my business, and therefore, I am exempt from the Dodd-Frank Act; the mistake was not considering that the Dodd-Frank Act could govern my seller. In a Subject-To transaction, one inherits more than just the mortgage—one also inherits good and bad opportunities. For example, one could inherit equity, cash flow, and depreciation, as well as tax liens, judgments, and HOA (homeowners' association) liens. Under these circumstances, one might understand how these mistakes could be made.

I reviewed my options and started to think creatively. There were solutions to this dilemma, and I wanted to find the one most suitable. One solution would be to get a hard money loan and take out a first mortgage. That would have required additional capital and severely impeded this property's tremendous cash flow. Another solution would be to get an investor loan from a traditional lending institution. Or I could find an investor to partner with me as a lender. They could pay off the mortgage, and then I would make monthly payments to them for a fair return on their money. The interest rate I would pay would be higher than "grandma's" interest rate, as she was an owner-occupant. Another possibility would involve finding an equity partner where I supplied the property, repairs, and property management in exchange for their dollars.

All these options would be viable solutions, but each would impede on my cash flow and profits. Was there a solution where I could still be the sole controller of the property? Then, after sleeping on it, the idea of buying on a Lease-Option hit me!

If I were to buy the house from her on a Lease-Option, I would lease the house for a period of time until exercising my option to buy it. And I would disclose to her that I would not be living in the property. So, for the lease option, I would not be an occupant; I would lease it to someone else. I went looking for a tenant-buyer, someone who would come and rent from me until they could get a loan and buy it—then we would wrap up the transaction. And this was actually the strategy that ended up working.

Karen was amicable. We explained to her and Judy the truth: this was an FHA loan, they changed the rules, we didn't know, but we're not walking away. We explained going forward on a Lease-Option and how it was a little different in that we don't get the benefits of ownership. When you do a Subject-To, there are tax benefits you receive because the title/deed is in your name. One of those advantages is that you get the benefit of depreciation; but that's a tax benefit we would not be able to get on a lease-option because we would be leasing and not owning. Everybody gets the interest deduction, and we were banking on the appreciation.

We were hoping that (over the next six months to a year or so) the property would go up enough in value so that we could sell it—and this would put a few bucks in our own pockets. We ended up leasing it for a year to a family who said they would eventually want to buy it; however, after that year, I guess they decided they didn't want to buy it, so they moved out. We then found another family who said that they wanted to buy it and would lease it from us until they got their finances in order.

We did another yearlong lease with them, and about eight months into it, something happened in their relationship, and they needed to move out. We were left with this property on our hands. We needed to get it back to being rent-ready, as well as carry out our evaluations as to whether we thought it was time to sell. Out of the blue, somebody just approached us. They saw one of our workers on the property and asked whether the house was for rent or for sale. They were then put in touch with us. They were a buyer and they had cash. We were able to put them in a position (using the same title company) where they were able to purchase the property.

We were able to make money on the property, in addition to the few dollars made during the previous eighteen months on the positive rent. And then, in about twenty-four months, the property sold, we made a profit, and as a show of good faith, we gave an additional $1,000 to the seller, Karen. She had no idea that was coming but we thought it was appropriate. Everybody came out a winner!

So, what we originally thought would be a good deal—taking it over Subject-To and then using it as a rental—ended up being a nightmare because we found out that with a government loan, it's now illegal to take over Subject-To. With some creative thinking, however, it turned out to a win/win, barely.

The solution to my nightmare:

1. Fully educated myself on the subject
2. Focused on positive, prosperous, viable solutions
3. Educated the seller on the dilemma and solution
4. Rewrote offer from "Subject-To," to a Lease-Option
5. Found tenant-buyer to purchase property within expiration of our option

As an investor, I thought the transaction was still a success. I controlled a property with very little initial cost. The buyer's money-down exceeded my out-of-pocket expenses. In addition, there was a terrific monthly cash flow. As a bonus, the property appreciated a few dollars due to an improving market, along with our updates and upgrades to the property. This experience taught me to inquire as to the type of loan when offering a Subject-To opportunity to a seller; also, I will always read the Title Commitment to confirm!

If you'd like to know what I can do for you and your Phoenix property, feel free to call me at (480) 443-4500, send an email to Stuart@Gethner.com, or visit my website, ContactStuart.com.

TOO MANY VISITS FROM GEORGE . . .

By
Michael Fitzgerald

Hagerstown

Every decade, the faces of most main streets change with the up-and-coming generation. The face of my hometown is still recognizable from when Union and Confederate soldiers shot black powder weapons in the streets. All our neighbors had stories of what happened. Some had homes with bullet holes or cannon balls stuck in the walls. Me, I didn't have a lot of time for stories. I was the oldest of six children, and we didn't have much; some might say we were underprivileged, but I might have considered that an upgrade. I watched my father work one-hundred-plus-hour weeks to support our family, and we still needed every anonymous charitable donation that showed up on our front porch. My father did what he could. We moved a lot. I went to five different elementary schools before we settled in historic Sharpsburg, Maryland.

It was hard watching my father work the way he did. Looking back, I think of it as a big part of my inspiration and drive. My mother says that by the time I turned six, she already saw it beginning, so when I asked at age twelve to start selling newspaper subscriptions, taking some of the family's financial responsibility into my own hands, it was hardly a surprise. I wanted only enough to take my brother and four sisters school shopping. Turns out I was pretty good. So good that I quickly sold over 1000 new subscriptions, and the local paper did a feature of me and my partner, Gideon, titled, "The Birdboy of Sharpsburg"—on account of Gideon being a white dove that rode on my handlebars as I peddled by bike through town.

I told the paper I had a plan to start a pet store and franchise it to people who wanted their own little slice of the dream. While I peddled around town selling news subscriptions, I drummed up every spare job a kid could find. I eventually started mowing lawns (up to fifteen a week), worked as a busboy (and graduated to a waiter at local restaurants), and worked in clothing stores—anything I could get my hands into, until I joined the army after graduating high school.

I spent three years in the 18th Airborne Corps out of Fort Bragg, North Carolina. After my military service, I found a professional-office gig, but wasn't satisfied. It made me restless, so I got on the Internet and negotiated a deal with a company in China to import thirty mini motorbikes, and I started selling them by word of mouth or passing out handwritten cards. With some cash in the bank, I decided to respond to a rent-to-own advertisement in the local newspaper.

The gentlemen on the other end of the line, Dave, commented that I sounded like I would do much better as a real estate investor than renting-to-own his home. He told me about the real estate associations in Washington D.C. and Baltimore. He also informed me that I could potentially purchase homes with no money down. Voted as "The Most Gullible Student" of my senior class, I naturally believed that I could purchase homes with no money. I attended several real estate association meetings, began networking, asking questions, and most importantly, I started taking action.

Within a couple of months, I purchased my first home with no money down, using a creative financing strategy known as a "division of proceeds." I renovated the home myself, maxing out every low-limit credit card in my pocket; I sold it for a quick profit; and I quit my job before the ink was dry. I never looked back. I closed on seventeen deals from my one-bedroom apartment including one that netted $1 million in equity through creative financing techniques.

Today, after thirteen years in business, I've been involved with over 1000 transactions, I have excellent relationships with local community banks, and my rental portfolio consists of 350-plus units. My company, Gideon Properties, is routinely involved in upwards of 100 transactions per year. Most recently, I've successfully renovated and revitalized two 50,000-square-foot office buildings in the heart of an up-and-coming downtown, which had previously gone ignored.

My company and I receive a lot of positive support from the community, with projects frequently featured in local news and magazine publications. I've received a citation from the governor of Maryland for my involvement in stabilizing the local downtown and doing business in the state. Anyone can do what they love, but not everyone can make money doing it. Investing gives me the opportunity to give back to my community. I routinely donate to many local charities, including providing wheelchairs to the disabled. I love what I do.

One of my proudest moments was the day I was able to purchase, renovate, and gift my childhood home back to my parents after it was lost to foreclosure. Overall, I enjoy giving back to my family and my community, spending time with my five-year-old son, making new friends, and volunteering on local boards and commissions. I love to travel, meet new people, and create an impact by taking action.

A Vacant Home

I received a lead from a couple—let's call them Brad and Janet—who'd been trying to sell a home on the market for two years. The home had started on the market at a decent opening price, and although they'd had several offers, they were unable to close. By the time they called me, they were asking well below what they owed. I knew the most I could give them would be an insult to them, so I held back from making an offer.

Considering the list price, it seemed impossibly low; but I could see from the photographs the house needed $60K in renovations and the neighborhood was subpar and getting rougher by the day. When I spoke to them, I explained that the home just wouldn't work, that I would love to buy the home, but it just wouldn't make sense for them. We want to buy properties where the homeowner wins and we can do something with the property, as well. I mean, it's not a deal unless it's a win-win, right?

To my surprise, Brad called me back and asked if I would be willing to give my advice on their home. It was an easy ten-minute drive from the office, so I agreed. The photographs hadn't done the place justice—and not in a good way. Sure the place had potential, even a touch of character; but I got a solid dose of reality when squatters started pouring out the back door, leaving behind a debris trail of various drug paraphernalia. This place had been vacant way too long!

Walking through the house I could tell it would need a thorough cleaning and paint, and in the basement, something would need to be done to fix the mold problem that had developed in the mother-in-law suite. Once I was done with my assessment, I did a three-way conference call with Brad and Janet to discuss the condition of the home. They asked whether they could have a formal sit down at my office and talk about their options. I agreed. At my office, I went through what they needed to do in order to sell the home on the market. My list was extensive.

Brad asked, "Mike, what would you buy the home at?"

I said, "Guys, I don't want to insult you with a low price. Brad, Janet, you owe a pretty penny on this home and you would have to take a considerable loss for me to purchase it. It's not a good deal for you unless you're winning, and I can win as well. The most I'd be able to pay for your property is well below your asking price plus closing cost. In its current condition, it wouldn't sell for much more on the market."

To my surprise they not only entertained the offer, they were willing to do whatever it took to get this property off their hands. After so many failed closings due to loan restrictions and cold feet, I couldn't blame them. Not to mention, they were living forty-five minutes away trying to run a farm. This home had become a burden for them and an eyesore to the community. As it turns out, you never really know how much the cure to a drawn-out headache is worth to a person. Still, our numbers were really far apart, and they would have to bring money to the table.

Fortunately, Brad's dad owned a 1000-acre farm, worth a few million with a large line of credit, and he agreed to lend Brad the difference for the closing. They were so happy when I agreed to buy it; I saw tears in their eyes, and they smiled ear to ear during the entire closing. Since I didn't have the restrictions that can come with many standard homeowner loans, there was nothing to prevent me from closing, and we were able to do so quickly. We stayed in touch, and a short time later, they did a testimonial about their experience—the ease of selling their property with an investor and how much they liked me. I even got a thank you letter.

Looking outside the box of conventional real estate transactions was vital for Brad and Janet. As with so many of my clients, the alleviation from selling a burdensome property feels like a gift for the people selling. I find it's as big a relief for their neighbors whose property values have dropped and who often had to contend with unsafe elements being drawn into an area populated with families and children.

On this one occasion, I began to sympathize with all those potential homebuyers who steered clear of this property. The original estimates came in around $60K. We thought we would update the home and sell it, with only four months invested. Boy, was I ever wrong; a can of worms popped out of every corner. First, the home had been divided into a duplex with three electrical meters. The upstairs was already a single-family home with a mother-in-law suite and/or extra unit downstairs. I thought I was just going to convert it into two meters and call it a day. Not so much. There was a local zoning rule where, if a home is vacant for more than a year, it is only allowed to be used as one unit with only one electrical meter. This was going to bump up my costs to $66K; but I'm an investor—I can handle a few upsets.

We continued forward making the change, unaware that we were required to have an electrical permit. After we got the meters done, we started working on the inside of the house, when an electrical inspector by the name of George showed up. He started his walk-through of the house, opening doors and closets. In the kitchen, he found a yellow wire hanging in the cupboard, dated 2007. He told me that although it was ten years old, there was no initial permit for that wiring, and it was like that when I purchased the home, I would have to pull the permit and fix it.

In addition, he said we needed to run new circuits for the preexisting outlets in the home because he felt there were too many on one circuit. He was also requiring us to eliminate the preexisting outlets in the basement that were above the baseboard heaters because they no longer met electrical codes. Due to the additional work for our electrician and drywall crews, we were looking at another hike in our renovation costs; but we moved forward to correct the issues. Thinking we had everything in order after a thorough inspection, we pulled the required permit and kept on working so that we could receive approval on our inspection. We were finally on the path to completion. Or so we thought . . .

George must have had a good time with the first inspection because he showed up for a second go-around. On his second inspection, he told us he felt the service cable to the home was toward the end of its life cycle, and he wanted it replaced. Now, since we had to replace the service cable to the home, we were also required to upgrade the copper grounding wire to the home. What could we do? The inspector knew what needed to be done, and we needed his approval to move on with this home, so we added in the additional cost and got to work.

To our utter dismay, George showed up a third time. It was starting to feel personal, as if he were going out of his way to make this as miserable a process as possible. George told us that, since we were doing more with the electrical than we originally planned (not by our choice), he was requiring us to replace the ten-year, sealed-battery smoke detectors—with hardwired smoke detectors at that! We were very frustrated, *Why didn't he bring this up on his first inspection?* He was the reason we were doing more electrical work in the first place. He was the head electrical inspector, so why did it take three inspections for him to "notice" all these "issues"?

Once again, we did all that was required of us—at a hefty cost from our contractors—we paid the reinspection fees, and called in for a final inspection. After all we'd been through, we felt we would pass this inspection and move on. George came in and told us everything looked good; but he felt some of the preexisting structure didn't meet codes. He wanted to call the building inspector to check the property before he would approve our electrical inspection. Why was he making assumptions outside of his duties?

The building inspector showed up to the property the next day to meet with our project manager and said that everything was fine with the home. We discussed some of our concerns, and he told us that he didn't know why George would tell us there were structural issues that needed to be fixed. George came back and finally issued our electrical approval. All of the changes George had required pushed my completion date way outside of my original timeline. At least I wasn't waiting to move my family into this place. It would have been a real challenge to someone in housing limbo. Inspection approvals in hand, we pushed forward to finish the renovations as quickly as possible in the hopes that we would finally get it completed, sold, and see a return on our investment.

Finally, I had a buyer on the line and under contract. I was excited to be coming to an end, and that all the time and work were about to pay off. That's when the other shoe dropped. To my complete surprise, I found out we couldn't have the mother-in-law suite in the basement. I'd need an engineer drawing and to have a set of stairs added in the house.

I didn't want to lose this buyer. I scrambled to get an engineer and tried with all my might to get everything taken care of in time for the closing; but it wasn't going to happen. Just like that, our buyer was gone, and we were another $30K over budget. I've never been so ready to through in the towel; but I am not a man who gives up so easily.

Enough was enough. I expected to have one or two things come out of an inspection. I could accept surprise inspections and hard-lined inspectors. Losing a buyer after I had the green light? I couldn't take that. I decided to contact the city and set up a meeting with the head inspector to explain all the hassle, all the back-and-forth, and all the lost time and profit I had to go through because the original inspector didn't tell me everything the first time. An inspection should not be an exercise in futility. He agreed, and I knew I was finally getting somewhere. We were able to work things out. I got the stairs installed, and we were done. A short time later, I found a new buyer and, to my relief, I squeaked a profit.

The Moral of My Story

Sometimes taking action isn't just about taking the course that's offered up to you. Sometimes you need to see what other options are available because, let's face it, the normal course just isn't working. Whether it's discovering that an investor is a better option for selling your home or finally deciding to take your case to the head inspector, it's about taking action.

No matter how frustrated you may get or how unfair things may seem, you just need to keep pushing forward. As long as you never give up and you keep momentum, you can always find the light at the end of the tunnel. Remember: Action + Action = Massive Results.

There is a lot to be said for a simple hassle-free sale. There's a great value in being able to sleep at night knowing your property is sold; that you won't have to worry about when or if it's going to settle; that you're going to get what you think you're going to get because you don't have to pay closing costs, inspection fees, or real estate commissions. There's a lot to be said for simple peace of mind. Sometimes taking the action of selling your home on your own will benefit you with bigger profits, and sometimes it will push you to your limits emotionally and financially.

Once again! *Action is key*. If you want to find out what a hassle-free sale of your Maryland property will mean to you, call me Michael Fitzgerald at (301) 960-4881, or email me at mike@gideonprop.com and experience the peace of mind a dedicated investor can provide.

When you're ready, the authors of this book came together to create just for you a 15-point checklist (with pictures) to help maximize your potential and profit in selling your house on your own. You can download a complimentary copy of, **"15 Must-Do Steps to Successfully Selling Your House On Your Own"**, at NoAgentNeeded.com

IT COULD ALL
BE SO SIMPLE

From Saving for Toys to Flipping Houses

By
Nasar El-arabi

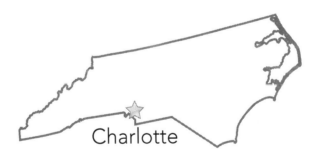

Charlotte

I've been an entrepreneur since I was about seven or eight years old. I started off just selling candy, making the effort to save some money. And I wanted to save that money to buy some Darkwing Duck toys.

I used to go with my parents to the doctor's office or wherever they went. If I saw any adults, I would approach them, saying, "Hey, do you want to buy some candy?" And I believe I would tell them it was a dollar. My parents encouraged me to save my earnings, and following their advice was the start of my career as an entrepreneur. In high school, I was the guy selling things out of his locker—whether it was white tee shirts, or video games, etc. Eventually, I went to college, which took me a little longer to finish than others, mainly because I didn't do what I was supposed to be doing. At nineteen, while I was home from college one time, I overheard my father talking to his friend about the guy next door who'd sold his house to an investor.

The investor showed up to the house with a brand-new Range Rover and a beautiful woman hopping out of the passenger seat; I was sold at that point. To put the icing on the cake, I heard my father telling his friend the investor bought that house for $150K, put $20K into it, and then sold it for $270K. On hearing those numbers, I was sitting there just thinking about that scene and calculating the profit—and I'm like, "Holy crap, that's a hundred grand!" I wanted to get started with real estate immediately. Me, being young (I mean, of course, if you want to get into real estate, the best person to ask is someone who does not do real estate—which was my father at the time); I asked him about it.

And he told me, "Hey, talk to my friend. He repairs credit. And maybe that'll help you out with, you know, buying a house."

My First Time Buying, Renovating, and Selling

So I started the process not of repairing my credit, but establishing it, because I was just nineteen. Eventually, in 2007, at the age of twenty-four, I bought my first house. So, eleven years ago, when there were "stated-income loans," I was approved for one because I have a pulse, and anybody with a pulse could get a loan at that time, if you recall. And with my first house, I attempted to actually buy, renovate, and sell—it was a disaster.

My partner and I pretty much did everything wrong. We watched *Flip That House* and all the other flipping shows and figured that we could do it, as if all we had to do was buy a house, yell at some contractors, and then make a bunch of money. I found the property via direct-mail marketing, the perfect house in the right neighborhood— or so I thought. I just knew I'd get my check and buy a Bentley GT coupe—while living at home with my father. Nothing could go wrong, at least that's what we thought, but it didn't work out like that.

We overpaid the contractor, who took advantage of us, and then took too long. We listed it too high, and at the end of the day, my partner and I ended up losing $7,000 each. So we lost $14,000 in all on that deal; but I still didn't give up on real estate at that point. I also finished college in 2007. After taking my defeat and eating my humble pie, I graduated, and in 2008, relocated to Charlotte, North Carolina. I ended up getting a 9–5 and buying rental houses on the side; through that 9–5, I was basically supporting myself.

After three months, I got a job installing cable. I lasted all of three weeks; climbing under houses and being handy was not for me. I got a call from a major Fortune 500 company to work in their call center, and I took the job; *Good-bye, Cable!* I was at their HQ making $12.50 an hour. While I was working there, I also bought a rental property in 2008, the traditional way—you know, through a real estate agent. And then, I bought another one in 2009.

Getting from the point where my 9–5 was funding my 5–9, to my 5–9 then being my 9–5 took some work. After that job, I went through similar jobs with a few other companies. Eventually, I needed to stop doing that line of work. I'll admit, I kept making errors; I was stressed out, and the stress was showing up in my face. My coworkers were concerned, and those who knew me kept asking whether anything was going on in my life.

When my 5–9 did become my 9–5, this was not an extremely hard transition for me; over time, I was able to paint my dad's house, and create a six-figure business by buying, renovating, and selling houses. Locally, I was able to meet some great people who mentored and coached me in the business. I was taught how to actually buy, renovate, and sell—the right way. Eventually, as with anything, I got better at it (your first house is normally your worst, but you do get better at it).

My company has purchased a lot of homes. It's not about the money with us as much as it was with me, initially; we try our best to go out and serve our clients and our community. When we provide a good service, we make money as a byproduct. As we all know, life happens, and it normally happens when we least expect it, or when we don't want it. We've had couples who need to relocate in thirty days, so they need to sell their house fast. We've also had people whose real estate agents would not list their house due to it needing so much work. My company is not here to put you out of your house; it's here to serve. We can buy your house fast or slow, it just depends on what the best solution is for your needs.

Selling for Retirement

One particular deal I came across in my career that really sticks out to me is a house we bought for $90K. The seller had multiple rental properties and wanted to retire. We contacted him through one of our direct-mail pieces. He did not want to do the necessary work on the house because it required a very extensive rehab. He'd had to evict the last tenants and just wanted to be done with it. My partner and I thought we'd just invest another $80K in it and then sell it around $230K. I called up one of my lenders, and he liked the neighborhood and the numbers, so he loaned us the money. We had six months to get it done, but once we bought the house, we realized the whole floor was rotten—the floor joists and everything.

Instead of spending $80K, we spent $130K due to the necessity of replacing the whole floor. I mean, we walked into the house and we could look down to see the dirt below—all of this, in and of itself, cost us an unforeseen $13K. We also needed to replace the water lines because the pressure was bad; this was an older house. Even after all of that, we then discovered the pipes outside the house were rotted and would not pass a homeowner's inspection; therefore, we had to replace the lines running from the sewer and water to our house.

And, of course, when the inspector came to inspect the floors, he found more issues. When a buyer purchases a house, they get an inspection report. The inspector is getting paid to find things wrong with the house—I mean that literally. Sometimes it can be a few hundred dollars in repairs and sometimes a few thousand. For example, if the inspector finds mold under a house, it's a possibility that the bank could pull funding from the buyer. I've seen people think they were selling their house and then, they found out they had tens of thousands of dollars in foundation issues.

One of the buyers wanted a survey done, and it was discovered that our property was six inches over the line into the next property. Before the bank could fund it, we had to get an ordinance from the city stating that it was grandfathered into a law because it had been built before X date. We were able to get that ordinance, so they did fund the loan, but we still had to basically redo the entire house. Our original budget was $80K, but then we spent $130K—we had to use $50K of our own money to get this done! After paying closing costs, money costs, and 6 percent real estate agent's commission, we broke even. It's all part of the business.

Lessons Learned

When you're buying, renovating, and selling a house, it's imperative to know you need to bring your house up to current standards. In working on getting these things up to that standard, my partner and I, of course, went over budget. So instead of making what we wanted to make, we ended up making just a little bit of money, and moved on.

With older houses, I've learned to always budget for all the plumbing and electric. If you choose not to, what normally happens is that these things come up when the buyer does their inspection to buy the house; the inspection report states that those things need to be changed, and the homeowner may choose not to proceed with the purchase without them. You know, sometimes flipping houses can just be a nightmare.

I now try to get all my loans extended to a year. I've learned that the most important part is not giving up, and also ensuring you have money saved up for things going wrong. It's known in the real estate profession: it's not *if* something goes wrong—it's *when* something goes wrong. If you are faced with challenges similar to my own, do not be afraid to tap out, sell it as is, and cut your losses early on. The only thing successful about this particular deal was getting each and every requirement done, as well as the real estate agent getting it sold. From that experience, I learned to be more careful in and out—and to not be afraid of crawling under the house.

Crawling under the house in order to see the rotten floor joist would have saved me $13K; I also would have seen how bad the plumbing and electrical was. Of course, you have to know what you are looking at to spot these things. If you're crawling under the house and you see dead rodents, that's definitely not a good sign. Call a professional pest-control company to remove everything because it will smell very badly.

My advice is that if you don't have money for unexpected issues, it's better to sell to guys who buy houses *as is* and let them deal with it.

Still, even with all the headaches, real estate has been great to me. I've been able to travel, take my father to the Super Bowl, and purchase my primary residence. Through all my mistakes, lessons, and opportunities, I actually wound up creating a pretty lucrative business by focusing on helping property owners.

Whenever you're ready to sell your house and you'd like to explore a fast and fair sale with my company, you can call me at (704) 268-9770, or visit my website at RealEstateBusters.com

THE LONG-DISTANCE SELLER

Moving Too Fast without Due Diligence

By
Raul Bolufe

I live in Miami, Florida. I started investing in real estate at twenty-one years old with the hopes of improving the quality of service for both buyers and sellers alike. Mainly focusing on wholesale real estate, I was able to grow my company from humble beginnings into a local, established brand. I quickly realized that being the best version of myself and, in essence, doing this for other people was not only my driving force but my ticket to success. Currently, I have some students whom I guide through the process with the ultimate goal of helping them grow their own businesses. Transaction after transaction, I discovered my passion for helping others achieve success in the industry, especially those starting from scratch like I did.

Having pursued an economics degree at Florida International University, I proceeded to engage in the exciting and fast-paced industry of investment real estate. Being passionate about looking for the best and most efficient ways to search for discounted deals and pass them along to investors so they can turn a profit, I was fueled up to progress as quickly as possible. At my present age of twenty-five, I've sold over 300 homes, and I own a small rental portfolio of single-family homes. I'm currently operating with a team of ten people and counting. I aim to constantly learn so that I may improve the way we help investors succeed in real estate investing.

Spring Hill, Florida

I found this deal through on online ad we posted on Google. We received an email and a call from Julie. She owned a rental property in South Florida. It was a really nice two-bed, one-bath property that she was renting out for $950 a month. Julie sent us pictures and quickly began to tell us she needed to sell quickly—within a week—because she needed the money to pay for law school. We took a look at the pictures and made a quick assessment. Julie told us the tenants were trustworthy and that the house was in pretty good shape. I immediately had a vision to purchase it and keep it in my rental portfolio. I was pumped!

Now the challenges we had here were that the property was three hours away from our office, the tenants were not easy to communicate with, and we had to close in less than seven days. My team and I were in for a treat. We had to rush the title company, and I had to gather all my money into my account in order to be prepared for everything—all of this in extremely little time and without me ever seeing the property in person or meeting our future tenants. Also, I didn't know any handypersons or contractors up there; if something went wrong, I would be in a deep hole—but I will get into that later.

Nonetheless, we gave Julie our word that we were purchasing this house, so there was nothing that would stop us. Fast-forward seven days and we closed! I couldn't believe it; after all the handwork, the finishing, and my team and I working diligently to close this, we actually did it. Then the fun began. Two days after closing, we received a call from the tenants with a two-page list of things that needed to be done to the house including the following:

- Electrical panel needed updating
- New water heater needed
- The pool was green (no chemicals could fix it)
- Two dump trucks worth of garbage
- Old appliances
- All the outlets needed replacing
- New Kitchen sink needed
- Plumbing work needed

The tenants started threatening to leave the house. This really brought my team together as we did our best to solve their problems, and ensure the house could be profitable. We are not in the business of losing money, and this was happening so fast.

Had I been aware of the issues that needed to be addressed at the beginning, I would have known these problems reduced the market value by over $20,000; this would have changed our offer substantially—not only because of the cost but also because of the time required to ensure the house would be in perfect condition. I don't believe Julie intended to put this burden on me because she didn't actually live near the property. Honestly, she did luck out on this because I took over all the headache and risk of something going really bad. That said, it was a great learning experience for me (and I hope it was for Julie as well) to be more in tune with whatever is happening in the properties you own.

To address everything on the two-page list, I went on Facebook and found a few guys to help my team. A week later, the tenant told us she was moving from the house. I quickly decided to sell the home, but I had to find an agent through a lot of networking and phone calls to list the property on the market. Thousands of dollars and three months later, I was able to sell the house and not lose any money.

In hindsight, it's clear to me that I did not do enough research on the house and tenants. Every house we buy is a different situation, and that's okay. It's actually my favorite part about this business; however, it is very easy to get in trouble and lose if you don't do the right diligence. I should have ensured that I spoke with the tenants and asked them whether everything was okay, and whether they were planning to stay longer. I should have paid for an inspector to go throughout the house and do a proper inspection. I should have tried to extend closing a little bit in order to get everything done.

Anyone can fall into these challenges the way we did, especially when they have a strong sense of service and integrity. I called the shot too early and said, "Julie, we are going to purchase your house in these seven days." And for anyone who doesn't know me, I do what I say, even if that means putting myself in a tight situation. I warn people—when buying from or helping sellers who are far from their backyard—to just take an extra day or two to do the proper research. It is real money and valuable time on the line, and we want to ensure that our client receives the service that we promise.

Closing the deal and getting the team on board (which consisted of my two office administrators, the title company, and my money partner) was what we did well, and this ultimately solved this challenge. We really are fortunate to have good people around us, people with high integrity. Collecting all the info needed to close was crucial for the title company and my money partner to set everything aside and work on this as quickly as possible. In the end, we closed on the deal as we said we would, Julie got her money and paid off her law school so she could continue with her life—and we did not lose anything in the transaction!

Problem:

Fast closing needed for seller in a property across the state

Solution:

1. Get our team on board and on the same page
2. Gather all information needed to close deal
3. Make sure money is available
4. Communicate with Julie (seller) daily until closing
5. Submit everything, send money, and close the deal

So, this is still a win in my book, especially for the learning experience of buying a property located in Spring Hill, Florida, with my office being three hours away in Miami. My team and I celebrated, even though it was nowhere near our greatest accomplishment. We were excited we were able to help Julie out, and that we left this deal with knowledge and some pretty awesome connections across town.

If you have a house in southern Florida that you need to sell fast, please contact me at (305) 507-4354 or raul@sellhousenowcash.com as I would be delighted to give you a fair and reasonable offer in as little as twenty-four hours. You won't have to fix a thing prior to your sale, and I'll even pay both of our closing costs. You can also visit my company's website at sellhousenowcash.com.

When you're ready, the authors of this book came together to create just for you a 15-point checklist (with pictures) to help maximize your potential and profit in selling your house on your own. You can download a complimentary copy of, **"15 Must-Do Steps to Successfully Selling Your House On Your Own"**, at NoAgentNeeded.com

CONCLUSION

S o there you have it. Some of the rise-and-fall-and-rise-again stories of some of the most successful real estate investors in the country. I hope you found some useful information, and that as you proceed with the sale of your property, you take what works and what fits, and you apply it, ignoring the rest. If anything, I hope you caught on to the running theme of each investor's story is that what seemed up front to be an easy opportunity can sometimes require a significant amount of effort and stress to achieve the desired result. Whichever approach you take to selling your house, you are now smarter for it. I wish you the best.

The intent of this book is to give you enough information to make an educated decision about whether selling your property with or without an agent would be the best fit for you. It really comes down to your deciding whether you want top dollar for your property or you want to sell it fast. The two outcomes typically don't go hand in hand. Also, they are derived from two different mindsets and approaches.

If you want to sell for top dollar, I would encourage you to consider working with, or at least interviewing, a local agent—and if you do hire them, to enable and empower them to do all the work for you. In my experience working as an agent and working as a real estate investor (who works with agents), the time and the effort required to properly prepare, market, show, negotiate, and close the sale of a property is typically not worth the time and energy it takes the nonexpert—there are more valuable things you could do with your time.

Here's what I mean, for starters: to get top dollar for a property, you'll need to walk through and analyze other properties for sale in your area (i.e. your competition). You'll need to take note of their condition. If you want to compete and sell for the same price or greater, you'll likely need to do some repairs, and potentially remodel all or parts of your property. If you want more from the sale, you might need to put a little bit more into the property prior to sale, while keeping your eye on that fine line of diminishing returns. Once you're prepared for market, you'll want the maximum number of eyes on your property in the interest of creating a bidding-war, which is typically the type of environment that will get you the maximum dollar allowed by the market. You'll need to properly position the pricing, launch a marketing campaign, and then prepare yourself to field, manage, and negotiate offers from both private buyers and agents alike. Yep, mostly agents.

Overall, what you'll actually need is the cooperation of real estate agents. Still to this day, 95 percent of all transactions are conducted with a real estate agent involved, meaning the real estate agents are essentially the gatekeepers to the buyers. Even if you haven't hired an agent, you will still need the cooperation of agents to market your property to the maximum number of buyers. And here's why . . .

With the advent of the Internet and technology, and all the information that is freely available to the average consumer, at the end of the day, when it's time for buyers to make their decision, they call an agent, because they want the agent to handle the transaction. They want the agent to conduct negotiations and process the paperwork.

Buyers would rather avoid the awkwardness of dealing with a seller face-to-face, while ensuring all the I's are dotted, all the T's are crossed, and that everything is done correctly, so that they can move into their new home. And they want to sleep well at night, and rest easy, knowing that everything was done to the letter of the law. Buyers want to know everything was done ethically and morally, and they also want to be sure that they themselves did nothing wrong, mistakes were not made, and they will not be taken advantage of.

If you want top dollar, that's essentially what it takes. If you want or need to sell fast, I'd ask you to consider looking at different real estate investors such as the professionals in this book —perhaps these very ones! These investors represent many different regions of the country, so much so, that one is likely convenient to you and your location. Consider calling them up and seeing what type of offer they can extend to you. You won't get top market dollar; but you will receive a fair offer that takes into consideration the time, effort, and expense it would take to get "top market dollar," which frequently equates to "top market *profit*."

Would you rather have the fast nickel or the slow dime?

That question really just boils down to what your time is worth. Do you need to get across the country because you just got a job transfer? Or did you just lose your job and you won't be able to afford that next mortgage payment? Did you inherit a property that you don't know what to do with? Have you reached your limit dealing with deadbeat tenants? Are you dealing with a personal emergency and need a large chunk of fast cash? Are there issues with the property structurally that you don't want to take the time, or you don't know how, to fix?

All of these aspects are different things to consider as to why you might need to sell fast, even if it is at a discount. It's really tough to place a value on "peace of mind," and taking a small haircut on the sale of a property might be worth it. Life happens to everyone. The good news is that whatever you might be going through that has you even considering selling your property quickly at a discount, it's temporary; and the time saved right now commonly ends up increasing your bottom line in the long run.

If you choose the path to the slow dime, be careful to not trip over the dollars to pick it up.

If you have any questions or concerns, you can go to the websites referenced inside of this book in multiple chapters and pages, and reach out to the people closest to your property's market. Ask them their opinion and their advice. That's why they contributed to this book, to help.

My colleagues are very service oriented. They are professionals, and they are helpful. They are real estate investors, and although they are in the business to make a profit, it is not their biggest goal. Their biggest goal is to make sure they don't lose, and when they can, to create win-win scenarios for situations like yours. More times than not, we find that the best option for people, in the long run, is to move along and get into their next chapter—into a full life. That's it. Good luck. God Bless.

When you're ready, the authors of this book came together to create just for you a 15-point checklist (with pictures) to help maximize your potential and profit in selling your house on your own. You can download a complimentary copy of, **"15 Must-Do Steps to Successfully Selling Your House On Your Own"**, at NoAgentNeeded.com

---

AUTHOR CONTACT INFORMATION

Billy Alvaro
Long Island, NY
631-400-EASY(3279)
EASYSELL411.com

Greg Zytkowski & Russell Taylor
Columbus, OH
(614) 468-5428
www.frepartners.com

Jeff Garner
St. Louis, MO
314-333-5555
www.StartingPointRE.com

Jason Hollon
Birmingham, AL
205-390-1050
www.WeBuyBham.com

Parker Stiles
Atlanta, GA
www.BarringtonHomeBuyers.com

Jeremiah Johnson
Wichita, KS
316-536-0132
www.FriendlyHomeBuyer.com

Paul Thompson
Little Rock, AR
paul@wincorehomes.com
www.wincorehomes.com

Todd Toback
San Diego, CA
(619) 365-4721
www.getitdonehousebuyers.com

Drew Hitt
Virginia Beach, VA
Drew@HamptonRoadsCashHomeBuyer.com
www.HamptonRoadsCashHomeBuyer.com

Omar Merced
Las Vegas, NV
(702) 706-7160
www.RealEstateWishes.com

Stuart Gethner
Phoenix, AZ
(480) 443-4500
ContactStuart.com

Michael Fitzgerald
Hagerstown, MD
(301) 960-4881
www.GideonProp.com

Nasar El-arabi
Charlotte, NC
(704) 268-9770
www.RealEstateBusters.com

Raul Bolufe
Miami, FL
(305) 507-4354
www.sellhousenowcash.com

Made in the USA
San Bernardino, CA
06 December 2018